Frankenstein – A Critical Study Guide

Edited by

Olympus Grove Press

Tinfish Type - Librarie du Levant 2015 - Marlinspike 25933

Frankenstein – A Critical Study Guide

Contents

This study guide is designed to support a student's reading of Mary Shelley's *Frankenstein*. It includes reference to the Gothic genre, historical context, major themes, contemporary critics, key quotations, essay questions and a model answer. There are revision notes included towards the end of the guide, giving a brief summary of all the major points, and near-contemporary responses to the novel.

PART ONE – CRITICAL GUIDE

Introduction

The moral lesson within *Frankenstein*, according to the critic Maurice Hindle, is that pride must have its fall. This is emphasized in the 1823 stage production's title: *Presumption; or The Fate of Frankenstein.* However, there's a great deal more to consider when studying a novel which is full of contradictions and thus open to interpretation. For some Victor's quest for 'the spark of life' is a noble ambition, for others he trespasses on the divine and, with the creation of his 'filthy' replica, creates a shady double.

At the beginning of her epistolary novel Victor Frankenstein has played God and Mary Shelley signals the significance of this to her reader with her subtitle and her epigraph. The subtitle - The Modern Prometheus - refers to the classical myth of Prometheus. In the Greek myth Prometheus taught man to hunt, read, and heal their sick, but after he tricked Zeus into accepting poor-quality offerings from humans, Zeus kept fire from mankind. Prometheus took back the fire from Zeus to give to man. When Zeus discovered this, he sentenced Prometheus to be eternally punished by fixing him to a rock of Caucasus, where each day an eagle would peck out his liver, only for the liver to regrow the next day because of his immortality as a god. He was intended to suffer alone for eternity, but eventually Hercules released him.

Prometheus was also a Roman myth, but with a very different twist. In this version Prometheus makes man from clay and water, again relevant as Victor rebels against the laws of nature (how life is naturally made) and as a result punished by his creation.

The epigraph in the novel is taken from Milton's *Paradise Lost*:

Did I request thee, Maker, from my clay
To mould me Man? Did I solicit thee
From darkness to promote me?'

The reference to Prometheus and the allusion to Lucifer and Adam are included at the beginning as each share a history of rebellion, a desire to 'steal' some of the sacred fire of life or knowledge for themselves.

Thus, in this seminal text, creation lies in the hands of God/Nature, but the blasphemous scientist, at least to most nineteenth-century readers, tries to interfere in this process. Yet Shelley also shows the student of natural philosophy questioning the principle of life: 'Whence, I often asked myself, did the principle of life proceed?' Frankenstein is a young idealist who believes in his goals and will go to any lengths to achieve them. His noble albeit self-serving intention is to rid the world of death, to 'renew life where death had apparently devoted the body to corruption.'

By examining the consequences of Victor's ambition, the author questions the goal of science itself: is science a way of improving life, or does it threaten our very existence? Shelley is likely to have acquired some of her ideas from Humphry Davy's book *Elements of Chemical Philosophy*, in which he had written that 'science has... bestowed upon man powers which may be called creative; which have enabled him to change and modify the beings around him'. Also amongst her contemporaries was Giovanni Aldini who made many public attempts at human reanimation through bio-electric Galvanism in London from 1801 to 1804. In her novel Shelley therefore explores the theme of playing God in a society in which man is constantly making 'progress,' or technological advancement. Science appears as a saviour yet usurping God in the novel leads to chaos and death.

Moreover, Frankenstein's creation is unnatural and the Creature is at first nothing more than a collection of body parts. The natural process of procreation and birth is shown as obsolete, yet with this comes the loss of maternal love.

Nevertheless, the rejected Creature, in keeping with Rousseau's view of man, is initially good. He only turns into a 'monster' after his love is not reciprocated, thereby demonstrating that monsters are shaped and created by their environment and their experiences in life. In other words it is nurture not nature which creates the monster.

Narrative Voice

The framing narrative of Walton, the shifting narrative perspectives and the use of multiple first person narrative voices are defining features of this epistolary novel. Like the Creature, the novel itself is made up of many parts, including other texts, and exceeds the ownership of any one individual. In spite of its title, *Frankenstein* refuses to be solely Victor's story and, 'Of component parts animated', it communicates through a variety of voices. We therefore see the move from individual to multiple competing voices in the structure of *Frankenstein* and the early conventional letter form (popular in the mid-eighteenth century) is transformed into the more familiar novel.

Shelley, within Walton's letters incorporates direct speech and his writing has a literary quality which elevates it above that of most correspondents. At the end of Walton's fourth letter, just before we begin Victor's account in Chapter 1, Shelley gives the reader, which in the text is Walton's sister, Margaret Saville, an account of how he will transcribe the story he is about to relate:

I have resolved every night, when I am not imperatively occupied by my duties, to record, as nearly as possible in his own words, what he has related during the day. If I should be engaged, I will at least make notes. This manuscript will doubtless afford you the greatest pleasure; but to me, who know him, and who hear it from his own lips - with what interest and sympathy shall I read it in some future day! Even now, as I commence my task, his full-toned voice swells in my ears; his lustrous eyes dwell on me with all their melancholy sweetness; I see his thin hand raised in animation, while the lineaments of his face are irradiated by the soul within.

Strange and harrowing must be his story, frightful the storm which embraced the gallant vessel on its course and wrecked it - thus!

The tale is written out after darkness has descended, which is fitting for a story which deals with a Creature that becomes synonymous with the night. It is likewise fitting, considering the maritime lexis Walton has employed in his letters, that he should metaphorically refer to Victor in his last paragraph as a 'gallant vessel' which has been wrecked by an, as yet, undisclosed force. Margaret Saville is thus given the means by which the story will unfold and a vivid representation - both aural and visual – of Victor, the primary storyteller.

After Victor's narrative has begun (when he becomes the autodiegetic narrator – the protagonist who narrates events) there is little mention of Margaret Saville, though towards the end of the novel Walton includes a direct appeal to his sister. The question he asks is no doubt one the writer, Mary Shelley, also wishes to ask her reader, her intention having been to 'awaken thrilling horror':

You have read this strange and terrific story, Margaret; and do you not feel your blood congeal with horror, like that which even now curdles mine?

Themes

An important theme is the creation of life, specifically Frankenstein's new, unnatural mode for 'creating' life. This mode of creation, involving neither God nor womankind, leads ultimately to destruction. There is no nurturing involved, and nature itself is manipulated, at least for the early nineteenth-century reader, in a diabolical way. This theme, of course, has become increasingly relevant with cloning procedures and

—

8

other technological advancements having raised questions about the ethics of mankind's involvement in 'creation.' Additionally, Frankenstein usurps the prerogative of creation not only from God, but also from woman and the novel abounds in depictions of familial relationships which shed light on Shelley's own family history: a woman's relationship to childbirth, a daughter's relationship to her mother, a daughter's relationship to her father.

The question of Victor's responsibility to the Creature is also one of the main themes of the book. When Victor saw the Creature come to life he fled the apartment, though the newborn Creature approached him, as a child would a parent. In February 1815, Mary Shelley had given birth to a baby two months prematurely, and the baby had died two weeks later. Some critics believe Percy Bysshe Shelley did not care about the condition of the premature infant and left with Claire, Mary's stepsister, with whom many believe he was having an affair. This obviously poses the question could Victor's reaction be based on Percy's abandonment of Mary and the baby?

Another theme is the human tendency/weakness to judge a person based on his/her appearance. It is true that the monster appears horrifying, but he is shown to be more 'humane' than the other humans; indeed, he is at first more sensitive and tolerant. Unfortunately, no one tries to understand him or to accept him the way he is. The nature of the human individual and the basic issue of inherent goodness or evil concerned many artists and thinkers of the Romantic age.

Furthermore, Shelley explores the theme of love, though it is the absence of love that is most striking. It is, after all, Victor's inability to love his creation and his refusal to make a partner for the Creature that generates the hatred and brings destruction down on his head. Therefore the lack of love between the creator and his creation leads only to misery and destruction. Likewise Victor's desire for Elizabeth is problematic and tainted with incest with the protagonist 'disturbed by the wildest dreams' about her: 'but as I imprinted the first kiss on her lips, they became livid with the hue of death.' After becoming a corpse, Elizabeth then transforms into Victor's deceased mother: 'I held the corpse of my dead mother in my arms; a shroud enveloped her form, and I saw the grave-worms crawling in the folds of flannel.' He wakes from this prophetic dream of death to a Creature assembled from the dead.

Whilst dreams and death themselves are explored in the work of many Romantic writers, *Frankenstein* also links them to eroticism. Victor's dream begins with an embrace and a kiss, a kiss which represents the doomed wedding night inasmuch as it seems to cause her death, much as his intimacy with Elizabeth leads to her being a victim of revenge. Here is the suggestion of incest: Victor's adopted 'more-than sister', metamorphoses after the dream-kiss into his mother. Whilst Elizabeth and Victor are not related, there are enough references to her as a sister to suggest a sexual taboo here, especially considering her transformation into his mother. This combines with the disturbing link between sex and death to present the protagonist as monstrous, despite his own view of himself as victim.

Dreams, a typical Romantic interest, play their part within *Frankenstein* and, coupled with the power of the imagination, can be seen as a significant theme within the novel. For example, whereas Percy Shelley, in his preface, tries to justify the work by highlighting its focus on science and its place in society, Mary Shelley was more concerned with the power of the imagination and the dream during the rainy summer of 1816 that inspired the tale: When I placed my head on my pillow, I did not sleep, nor could I be said to think. My imagination, unbidden, possessed and guided me.' Mary Shelley therefore presents herself as the recipient of the story rather than the creator, as if she has been transported by an imaginative power beyond her control.

Another theme worth mentioning is friendship, or the lack of it. From the outset, as early as Walton's second letter, it is clear that isolation and solitude are key themes. 'I have no friend', Walton complains, a sentiment that is echoed throughout the novel. The use of three separate first-person narrators could be seen to heighten this, with each locked in his own way of seeing and sense of despair and separation from others. And perhaps it is also worth comparing Victor Frankenstein to the sociable Clerval, a comparison which highlights the potentially negative consequences of the isolated and obsessive Romantic figure.

With its focus on male friendship *Frankenstein,* for many critics, is largely about men and men who are insensitive to women or the realms traditionally associated with them: home; family, motherhood etc. Some have noted how the novel seems to suggest how destructive it can be if male values come to dominate. The women, while being beautiful and warm, are proved largely ineffective and are in the main victims. Even the Creature is denied a mate.

In conclusion, *Frankenstein* is a key Gothic text which explores many familiar themes and is very much concerned with late Romantic interests and ideas and yet, with its re-animation of body parts, it is also one of the earliest examples of science-fiction. Shelley therefore explores Romantic and scientific concerns with great inventiveness and uses the one to develop the other.

Structure

When looking at the structure of *Frankenstein*, questions of narrative authority immediately confront the reader. The text has a tangled story line and because of the triple narrative and an elaborate series of parallel personalities and events we wonder just whose story we are hearing. Is the Creature's tale a projection of Frankenstein's tormented psyche or a brutal condemnation of the vain, ambitious and insensitive male creator?

This complex structure involves a series of framed or embedded narratives. The framing narrative is Robert Walton's as he describes his attempt to reach the North Pole and his encounter with Victor Frankenstein. Within this relatively realistic layer Victor tells Walton the story of how he created and abandoned the Creature and the revenge it took upon him by destroying those he loved most. Further narratives can be found within Victor's account in the letters from Elizabeth, who was taken in by the Frankenstein family and whom he intends to marry, and from his father. In the central narrative, the Creature then challenges Frankenstein's account of events as he describes the development after his flight, and his experiences of rejection. Within this story we also learn about the history of the De Lacey family and of Felix De Lacey's betrothed Safie.

In addition to all of these narratives, there are numerous references to extra-textual narratives, including Samuel Taylor Coleridge's *The Rime of the Ancient Mariner* (1798), another tale of an alienated individual and the disturbance of natural order. Out of the three books the Creature discovers in the woods arguably the most important of these is Milton's *Paradise Lost* (1667), which provides both an epigraph for the novel and a framework through which both the Creature and Victor understand their changing situations.

When considering the structure of the novel we must also consider uncertainties which affect the reliability of the multiple narrators. Walton conveys Victor's narrative (written up from notes, which are then amended by Victor himself); Victor transmits the Creature's, presumably rendering it into English from the original French; the Creature transmits that of Felix and Safie, deriving it partly from their love letters. Hence, at the heart of this Gothic tale is an epistolary love story which we cannot read. Safie's letters were dictated in Turkish to a bilingual servant, who translated them into French for Felix's benefit. The Creature, from his spy-hole, makes copies of these, which he presents to Victor, assuring him that 'they will prove the truth of my tale'. Yet we have no description of these copies.

Finally, it is worth saying that in keeping with all good stories *Frankenstein* takes its main characters through dramatic arcs. At the start, Victor is in control. He is educated and has a glittering future before him and then we get the chance to witness his gradual reduction to a gibbering wreck. The

Creature too begins life quite auspiciously in nature but then begins a rapid decline into fury and revenge largely due to the reception he receives at the hands of the De Lacey family and Victor.

Form

The epistolary novel had fallen out of fashion by the time Mary Shelley had started writing *Frankenstein*. However, the letter form arguably gives the novel a degree of verisimilitude which such a fantastical tale needs if it is to be believed. Therefore, in keeping with a legend's attempt at veracity through attention to natural details, Shelley seeks realism through epistolary and documentary styles. In *Frankenstein* there are the journal-like letters of Captain Walton sent to his sister which contain the further narratives of Frankenstein and the Creature and the entire book is 'addressed' – literally, as letters – to a woman reader who is absent, but who is also present because she is half of the dialogue (with her omitted responses to Walton's letters). Throughout *Frankenstein* we are frequently reminded that we are reading. This is typically accomplished by our attention suddenly being drawn to its form, pulling the reader away from the 'action' through emphasizing that this is a told and recorded narrative. For example, just before he recounts the Creature's first murder – at a moment when tension is building – Victor interrupts himself to address Walton directly: 'I fear, my friend, that I will render myself tedious by dwelling on these preliminary circumstances'. The presumptive reader's presence, our avid involvement in a suspenseful narrative, is teasingly evoked by Victor's ironic apology to Walton for 'tediousness'.

Setting

The Arctic is not usually thought of as a Gothic setting, yet an inhospitable, hostile environment where ruined castles are replaced with rugged mountains of ice serves its purpose as the location for the recording of the intertwining stories. Locked as they are in the ice north of Archangel anything could happen.

Furthermore, the novel's settings would have spoken directly to some of the most compelling aspects of early nineteenth-century culture such as the fascination with exploration both scientific and geographical. For example, the Alps – site of Victor's encounter with the Creature – were of particular interest. Mont Blanc had only recently (in the 1780s) been climbed and the geological and botanical investigation of that region was the source of all sorts of scientific treatises and narratives.

There are also the sublime landscapes to consider from a Romantic perspective. The mountains of Switzerland inspire awe and nature itself is frequently championed as a positive force. The philosopher Jean Jacques Rousseau's most famous dictum, 'man is born free but everywhere finds himself in chains', promotes the idea, which Shelley appears to be in agreement with; that it is only in nature that human beings can be most true to themselves and it is when they encounter civilisation that they become corrupt.

Denouement

At the end of Victor's narrative, Captain Walton resumes the telling of the story. A few days after the Creature's initial appearance the ship becomes trapped in pack ice and Walton's crew insists on returning south once it is freed. In spite of a passionate speech from Frankenstein, encouraging the crew to push further north, Walton realizes that he must accede to his men's demands and agrees to head for home. Frankenstein dies shortly thereafter.

Walton discovers the Creature in his cabin, mourning over Frankenstein's body. Walton hears the Creature's reasons for his vengeance and expressions of remorse. Frankenstein's death has not brought him peace. Rather, his crimes have increased his misery and alienation, and his words are almost exactly identical to Victor's own in describing himself. He vows to kill himself on his own funeral pyre so that no others will ever know of his existence. Walton watches as he drifts away on an ice raft that is soon lost in darkness, never to be seen again.

In some ways the novel avoids closure: Walton's expedition is cancelled, Victor dies without revenging himself upon his creation, and the Creature floats away into the darkness. For some readers such open-endedness gives the novel an unsatisfactory conclusion yet this is partly due to a Romantic sensibility that favours uncertainty over authority. To give it a tidy ending would be to diminish its power to make us think about the issues it raises. *Frankenstein* deals with dreams and death, isolations and oppositions and, ultimately, free will. Victor's removal from society is his own choice whereas the Creature's isolation is a forced one.

Language

With 'a hand *seemingly* stretched out to detain' we are given Victor's response to the Creature when it first appears in its animated state. The key word here, of course, is *seemingly*. This adverb gives the reader room to doubt Victor's interpretation of the act. Was the Creature seeking to detain him, or was it reaching out for help?

Readings and misreadings are intertwined within each narrative, though words in the Gothic often fail the narrator at key points. For example, Victor's 'no mortal can describe the horror of that countenance' is a Gothic device frequently used.

When looking at language we must also consider the use of names. The name Victor implies that the character aspires to be famous. It has a Latinate dignity, suggesting he is destined to be victorious and be commemorated in stone, though in his Promethean attempt to be immortalised Frankenstein breaches sacred boundaries.

Unlike Victor, the Creature has no name but is referred to, with the use of a suitably Gothic register, as 'wretch', 'daemon', 'fiend', 'demoniacal corpse' and 'monster'. Recounting the night of the Creature's 'birth', Victor speaks of the 'hard' breathing and 'inarticulate sounds' with which the Creature attempted communication. But this character is one who, when he has the opportunity to address his creator, greets Victor's hysterical ravings with the calm 'I expected this reception'.

The beauty of the Creature's eloquence, his clarity and calmness of communication strike us powerfully because they contrast so starkly with Victor's panic-stricken abuse. Victor's 'Begone, vile insect! or rather, stay, that I may trample you to dust!' show his own uncertainty, and serves to highlight the Creature's polished presentation of his requests. Indeed, there is such a gulf between the two that it becomes clear that Shelley is inviting the reader to reassess all that they have been told up until this point.

During their first exchange the Creature's use of archaic and formal language is also surprisingly moving, and elevates his diction above that of Victor's, who struggles to communicate coherently. The Creature controls the exchange, his dialogue being not only more sophisticated, but also more sustained: he speaks over eight hundred words while Victor manages only just over two hundred. Where his Creature speaks in fluent and complex sentences, Victor's contributions are full of exclamation marks and fractured clauses. Thus the Creature brings one chapter to a close, seizing control of the narrative in a most unexpected manner, and revealing his true articulate self to his creator and, more importantly, the reader.

Victor Frankenstein

Victor, with his appreciation of the sublime and his interest in science and philosophy, is similar in many ways to Percy Bysshe Shelley, and Mary's own sympathies, at least in the first edition (publ.1818) lie with Victor - a name Percy was known to have preferred to his own. But her initial sympathy for the Romantic hero wanes, and in the longer second edition (publ.1831) she clearly feels a greater degree of sympathy for the Creature.

Victor, in the second edition (and the one I/GCSE and

A Level students study) proves himself to be monstrous in a number of ways. He craves solitude, shunning the society of men; for science and fame he undertakes the most gruesome of tasks: pillaging charnel houses, stitching limbs together; and arguably proves himself the least humane character in his rejection of his child.

As a scientist Victor represent the rational and the threats of modernisation, but he also embodies, like Percy Bysshe Shelley, the Romantic rebelliousness towards accepted modes of thought in his pursuit of forbidden knowledge, and this sets him apart from other men. Thus he is also a Romantic and isolated figure. His ambition to create life from death is often attributed as the cause for his neglect of family and friends while at university, but he admits earlier that 'two years passed… during which I paid no visit to Geneva' and we are told it is his temper 'to avoid a crowd'. He goes on to spend his time alone with only the dead for companionship. 'In a solitary chamber… separated from all the other apartments'. Victor works in self-imposed isolation, an outsider by choice, and thus so very different from the Creature of his making. Only when his studies are complete does he think of returning home, but then he is again distracted by a personal pursuit that 'caused me also to forget those friends who… I had not seen for so long'.

Furthermore, Victor animates dead tissue and creates life without the biological aid of a mother, and rather than respond with care towards the 'child', he flees from the responsibility. If we consider the love and support he himself received this again sets Victor apart from others. His creation is abandoned and left to fend for itself.

Victor, having abandoned his responsibilities, travels into the countryside where the serenity of the 'majestic' surroundings contrasts greatly with his troubled mind. These grand examples of the natural world, the mountains, the ravine, the glaciers, are again typically Romantic and they serve to emphasise the unnatural pursuits of Victor in trying to 'penetrate the secrets of nature' and plundering 'her hiding-places'. Though he is like many other scientists, he is the only one whose metaphorical rape of the natural world has resulted in creating life.

Victor, therefore, is a somewhat vain, self-obsessed and deeply flawed Romantic hero and some critics have likened him to Milton's Satan: the lonely individual who sees himself as heroic in some way and who feels he has to battle against all sorts of odds to achieve something which turns out to be nothing more than a pyrrhic or hollow victory.

In conclusion we can say that his suffering is self-inflicted, and this is something which he intermittently acknowledges: 'I have drawn down a horrible curse upon my head.' By choosing to create a 'wretched Creature' the ambitious scientist chooses his own fate.

Henry Clerval

Henry Clerval is the son of a Genevese merchant. He is a 'boy of singular talent and fancy', is 'deeply read in books of chivalry and romance' and is able to call forth the 'better feelings' of Victor's heart. Like Victor, he 'loved enterprise, hardship, and even danger for its own sake' However, rather than being drawn to science Clerval spends his youth composing heroic songs and writing tales of enchantment and knightly adventure. Victor recounts that Clerval 'tried to make us act plays and to enter into masquerades, in which the characters were drawn from the heroes of Roncesvalles, of the Round Table of King Arthur, and the chivalrous train who shed their blood to redeem the holy sepulchre from the hands of the infidels'. Clerval occupies himself with the 'moral relations of things...the virtues of heroes' and can therefore be seen as a character who differs in many ways from Victor. For some critics he is the ideal Romantic poet. Yet Clerval, in keeping with Walton and Victor, hopes 'to become one among those whose names are recorded in story as the gallant and adventurous benefactors of our species'.

The Creature

Mary Shelley famously described the novel in 1831 as 'my hideous progeny' and her second edition of *Frankenstein* (publ.1831) clearly identifies with and invites sympathy for the Creature, allowing him to speak and to explain his monstrous behaviour.

Within the Creature's words, both as he confronts Victor for the first time, and in his description of his growing consciousness, there is a musicality, in that he creates images of great beauty and scenes of great pathos. He tells of his fear at 'finding [himself] so desolate', describing himself as 'a poor, helpless, miserable wretch'. He knows nothing, not even the basest of sensations, and his first experiences are of what he later learns to call pain. As he crawls into existence he proves himself to be a Creature of great sensitivity and quickly learns to distinguish the 'harsh notes' of the song of the sparrow from the 'sweet and enticing' song of the blackbird and the thrush.

The Creature, with its eloquent defence, represents Rousseau's Noble Savage, but it also comes to symbolise the fear of the mob, the bloodletting of the French Revolution, and, from a psycho-analytical perspective, Victor's tainted soul (the fiend that lurks in his heart, hence his doppelgänger). Yet even within Victor's narrative, the reader is drawn towards the Creature because of its treatment (remember it saves a child and then is punished) and we are surprised by the Creature's biblical register shaped by its reading of Milton. (It is worth noting his eloquence is lacking in Whale's 1931 film with the mute - albeit equally victimised - monster.)

The Creature in the novel, with its natural innocence and child-like wonder, is also a passive, grateful absorber of nature's offerings. His ferocious rejection by the shepherd, then the children, then the woman, and finally an entire village reveals him to be the passive receptor for abuse and attack. And it is here that men, in Elizabeth's words, begin to prove themselves to be 'monsters thirsting for each other's blood'.

However, sympathy in the final chapter swings between Victor and Creature. The last word is the Creature's - though it is also worth remembering that in the penultimate chapter the Creature appears cruel (see the graveyard scene where he taunts Victor).

At the heart of the Creature's tragedy is the potential he had for great good – he brings firewood to the door of the de Lacey's home, he observes them, his instincts are loving instincts. Unlike orthodox Christian teaching that man is fundamentally flawed and sinful, the Creature isn't – it is innocent and good. Though later it becomes violent and vengeful, a childhood innocence influenced by events beyond its own control provides a particular pathos. Mary Shelley therefore gives the reader a Creature that is naturally benevolent and kind, but the actions done to it drive it to destruction. The tragic thing at the heart of the novel is that, with paternal love, there could have been such a very different outcome.

What to Call the Creature?

There is no doubt that there are aspects that are horribly monstrous about the Creature and so it is forgivable that we fall into calling him 'the monster'. The etymology of 'monster' reminds us that the word suggests something to be looked at (monstrare – Latin; demonstrate – English; montrer – French) and so supports our use of this label. Indeed, the Creature is remorselessly judged by his appearance. But, as with any sort of evaluative naming, the label insinuates certain things about the Creature's interior as well as his exterior being, and this is where we perhaps need to be more careful.

Externally, the being is certainly monstrous. Physically he is a vile assembly of ill-matching parts and even though each part is chosen for its beauty, the result is hideous:

His limbs were in proportion, and I had selected his features as beautiful. Beautiful! – Great God! His yellow skin scarcely covered the work of muscles and arteries beneath; his hair was of a lustrous black ...; his teeth of pearly whiteness; but these luxuriances only formed a more horrid contrast with his watery eyes ... his shrivelled complexion and straight black lips.

Furthermore, for practical reasons, Victor makes him significantly larger than the average human – he stands 'eight feet in height, and proportionally large'. Later we hear how the desperate Creature horrifies even himself when he first sees his reflection in a pool.

So what of the other labels one might use for this unfathomable character? Should we be led by the labels provided by our narrators: 'fiend', 'daemon', 'wretch'? The problem is that all of these nouns also carry value judgements. 'Fiend' suggests the devil, as does 'daemon', and 'wretch' only works in that the Creature is, for the most part, wretched. In conclusion, calling the character a 'Creature' seems fairest. It reminds us of the basic truth – that he is something that was created, albeit with the capacity to communicate effectively. We see him turn monstrous as a result of the damages inflicted by the monstrosity of our own world and through the neglect of his creator.

Women in *Frankenstein*

Victor: The saintly soul of Elizabeth shone like a shrine-dedicated lamp in our peaceful home. Her sympathy was ours; her smile, her soft voice, the sweet glance of her celestial eyes.

In *Frankenstein* the human female is often portrayed as passive and compliant, particularly in the heavily edited 1831 edition. Victor does not appear to be attracted to women and even when he marries Elizabeth he shows little of the passionate interest that he displays towards his scientific experiments. Although all of the females' roles are small it may be argued that the novel explores Frankenstein's fear of sexuality through his attempt to create a world that excludes women. It has been suggested Shelley is trying to show that if men continue to exclude women society will be less civilised or successful. Thus, despite writing about meek, subservient women Shelley is actually exploring radical, distinctly feminist ideas. Interestingly the only two females who are bestowed with independent behaviour are Safie and the unfinished female Creature.

From the beginning Frankenstein views Elizabeth as little more than a 'pretty present' to, 'protect, love and cherish.' In the 1818 edition Elizabeth craves self-improvement, but she becomes a patriarchal idealisation. It is interesting to note that Safie too is presented as a gift to Felix. *Frankenstein* takes this limited female role to an extreme by eradicating the need for a female in the reproduction of life. However, it is worth noting that even though he succeeds in creating life, Frankenstein rejects his child and therefore, undeniably fails as a parent.

Later in the novel Frankenstein justifies destroying the female Creature because of his fear that 'in all probability she was to become a thinking and reasoning animal who might refuse to comply with a compact made before her creation.' Victor views the female as capricious and is arguably afraid of independent, freethinking women - hence he destroys them.

Context

The initial part of *Frankenstein* began life in 1816, evolving from a ghost story competition among Byron's guests, Mary, Percy Shelley and Dr Polidori, at the Villa Diodati on the shores of Lake Geneva.

Below is Mary Shelley's description of how the novel came into being. Note the emphasis on the horror associated with man's blasphemous desire to create life (for a full account of the novel's origin see *The Life and Letters of Mary Shelley*):

'I saw the pale student of unhallowed arts kneeling beside the thing he had put together. I saw the hideous phantasm of a man stretched out, and then, on the working of some powerful engine, show signs of life, and stir with an uneasy, half vital motion. Frightful *must* it be; for SUPREMELY frightful would be the effect of any human endeavour to mock the stupendous mechanism of the Creator of the world.'

Mary Shelley was haunted by the blasphemous act and the fear that the novel would be condemned as sacrilegious. This is less of a concern for the modern reader who is unlikely to consider the usurpation of God's role as a serious issue. Today's reader is also less inclined to feel the horror Mary Shelley intended to awaken and less sympathy for the self-centred Victor. We may, however, feel more keenly the class prejudice the novel contains, the judgements based on nothing more than appearance, and Victor's failure as father; one who, ironically, willingly reflects on the 'golden' ties and 'silken cord' contained within his own childhood.

Other contextual factors to consider can be informed by biographical criticism. Mary Shelley wrote travelogues and Frankenstein's journey across Europe as a 'divine wanderer' is almost a low-spirited Grand Tour, a pilgrimage with no clear end. Furthermore, she went on to write the novella *Mathilda* between August 1819 and February 1820. It deals with the common Romantic themes of incest and suicide. The act of writing this short novel distracted Mary Shelley from her grief after the deaths of her one-year-old daughter Clara at Venice in September 1818 and her three-year-old son William in June 1819 in Rome. These losses plunged Mary into a depression that distanced her emotionally and sexually from Percy and left her, as he put it, 'on the hearth of pale despair'.

In the novella *Mathilda* the eponymous narrator tells, from her deathbed, the story of her unnamed father's confession of his incestuous love for her and his suicide by drowning. Her relationship with a gifted young poet called Woodville fails to reverse Mathilda's emotional withdrawal or prevent her lonely death. Some critics have read the text as autobiographical, the three central characters standing for Mary and Percy and her father, William Godwin.

Mary Shelley sent the finished *Mathilda* to her father

in England, to submit for publication. However, though Godwin admired aspects of the novel, he found the incest theme 'disgusting and detestable' and failed to return the manuscript despite his daughter's repeated requests. In the light of Percy's later death at 29 by drowning (1822), Mary came to regard the novel as ominous and it wasn't published until 1959. It's relevance to *Frankenstein* is perhaps only slight, yet it does foreground the theme of incest as one repeated within her writing and gives the critic, with the 1831 edition of Frankenstein, an insight into the mindset of the author who was all too familiar with death and suicide. (At this point it is worth reminding ourselves that Percy's first wife drowned herself in the Serpentine.) It is also worth noting that in the 1818 edition Elizabeth is actually related to Victor, being the only child of his father's sister and therefore his cousin.

Today *Frankenstein* is often read as an early science-fiction novel. For example, the science fiction writer and critic Brian Aldiss has argued that it should be considered the first true science fiction story because, in contrast to previous stories with fantastical elements resembling those of later science fiction, the central character 'makes a deliberate decision' and 'turns to modern experiments in the laboratory' to achieve fantastic results. For other critics it is a sophisticated and Romantic version of the popular and populist Gothic novel. Indeed, the Gothic shares so many Romantic concerns that it became common to distinguish between the two on grounds of readership; the Romantic was considered 'high' literature whereas the Gothic represented popular 'low' fiction, sensational in its use of the monstrous and macabre. As a result, the Romantic was often - and in some circles still is - used as a way of justifying a text's worth.

Intertextuality

The novel's three main influences are made clear from the beginning: its alternative title of *The Modern Prometheus* is late Neo-Classical or early Romantic in its use of classical myth, Milton's *Paradise Lost* is referred to at length, and similarities with Coleridge's *The Rime of the Ancient Mariner* abound.

Beginning with the Promethean myth it is easy to see how it came to overshadow the wet Genevan summer of 1816. Byron had recently written a poem called *Prometheus* and he and Shelley were reading the 5th Century BC playwright Aeschylus' *Prometheus Bound* after which – though it is hard to date that work precisely – Shelley produced a translation and went on to write one of his most ambitious poems *Prometheus Unbound.* Prometheus in the Greek myth, as mentioned in the Introduction, is a Titan – one of the earlier gods of Greek Mythology defeated by the Olympians. He sides with humankind against Zeus and supplies them with the knowledge of fire. His punishment is a terrible one: chained to a mountain top, his liver eaten each day by Zeus's eagle, growing back each night in time for the next day's ordeal. Prometheus is a heroic, thinking figure, who endured pain and suffering for humankind and Mary Shelley's subtitle is not without irony; suggesting we are to understand Victor to be some kind of latter-day Prometheus but a very flawed one. He may want to think of himself in Promethean terms but he does not merit it.

Mary Shelley's references to *Paradise Lost* serve to highlight both Victor's and the Creature's plight, though it is the Creature who appropriates both Adam and Satan within the text. John Milton's *Paradise Lost,* published in 1667, is an epic poem in blank verse and deals with the Fall of Man: the temptation of Adam and Eve by the fallen angel Satan and their expulsion from the Garden of Eden. Milton's purpose, stated in Book I, is to "justify the ways of God to men". The poem follows the epic tradition of starting *in medias res* (Latin for *in the midst of things*), the background story being recounted later. Percy Shelley notes in the preface to his lyrical drama *Prometheus Unbound* that he constructed his character Prometheus in part as an attempt to revise Milton's Satan.

Coleridge's *The Rime of the Ancient Mariner* is quoted by Walton when trapped in Arctic ice and, like Victor, the Ancient Mariner defies God. The poem was published in 1798 and relates the experiences of a sailor who has returned from a long sea voyage. The mariner stops a man who is on the way to a wedding ceremony and begins to narrate a story. The wedding guest's reaction turns from bemusement to impatience and then from fear to fascination as the mariner's story progresses.

Mary's father, although differing from Coleridge on key matters of philosophy and theology, was deeply attached to the poet and he was a frequent guest in the Godwin household. Mary Shelley never forgot the experience of hearing Coleridge recite his 'Rime' as she hid behind the sofa and the tributes to him in *Frankenstein* suggests a deep and personal admiration.

When dealing with intertextuality it is also mentioning *The Sorrows of Werter*. The German novel has a profound effect upon the Creature and it is worth considering the Creature's response:

'In *The Sorrows of Young Werter*, besides the interest of its simple and affecting story, so many opinions are canvassed and so many lights thrown upon what had hitherto been to me obscure subjects that I found in it a never-ending source of speculation and astonishment. The gentle and domestic manners it described, combined with lofty sentiments and feelings, which had for their object something out of self, accorded well with my experience among my protectors and with the wants which were forever alive in my own bosom. But I thought Werter himself a more divine being than I had ever beheld or imagined; his character contained no pretension, but it sank deep. The disquisitions upon death and suicide were calculated to fill me with wonder. I did not pretend to enter into the merits of the case, yet I inclined towards the opinions of the hero, whose extinction I wept, without precisely understanding it.'

The Sorrows of Young Werter (German: *Die Leiden des jungen Werthers*), is a loosely autobiographical novel (publ.1774) and considered an important text of the Sturm and

Drang period in German literature. It also went on to influence the later Romantic literary movement. Finished in six weeks of intensive writing during January–March 1774, its publication instantly made the 24-year-old Goethe one of the first international literary celebrities.

Like *Frankenstein*, the majority of *The Sorrows of Young Werther* is presented as a collection of letters written by Werther, a young artist of highly sensitive and passionate temperament, and sent to his friend Wilhelm.

In these letters, Werther gives an intimate account of his stay in a fictional village. He is enchanted by the simple ways of the peasants there. He meets Lotte, a beautiful young girl who is taking care of her siblings following the death of their mother. Despite knowing beforehand that Lotte is already engaged to a man named Albert who is 11 years her senior, Werther falls in love with her.

Although this causes Werther much anguish, he spends the next few months cultivating a close friendship with both of them. His pain eventually becomes so great that he is forced to leave. While he is away, he makes the acquaintance of Fräulein von B. He later returns to the village where he suffers more than he did before, partially because Lotte and Albert are now married. Every day serves as a torturous reminder that Lotte will never be able to return his love. Out of pity for her friend and respect for her husband, Lotte comes to the decision that Werther must not visit her so frequently. He visits her one final time, and they are both overcome with emotion after Werther's recitation of a poem.

Werther realises that one member of their love triangle has to die in order to resolve the situation. Unable to hurt anyone else, Werther sees no other choice but to take his own life. After composing a farewell letter to be found after his suicide, he writes to Albert asking for his two pistols, under a pretence that he is going 'on a journey'. Lotte receives the request with great emotion and sends the pistols. Werther then shoots himself in the head, but does not die until 12 hours after he has shot himself. He is buried under a linden tree, a tree he talks about frequently in his letters, and the funeral is not attended by clergymen, Albert or his beloved Lotte.

Napoleon Bonaparte considered it one of the great works of European literature. He thought so highly of it that he wrote a soliloquy in Goethe's style in his youth and carried *Werther* with him on his campaigning to Egypt. It also started the phenomenon known as the *Werther-Fieber* (Werther Fever) which caused young men throughout Europe to dress in the clothing style described for Werther in the novel. It reputedly also led to some of the first known examples of copycat suicide. The Creature in *Frankenstein* is greatly influenced by the novel (as seen in the extract) and this arguably sheds light on the Creature's intention at the end of the novel.

Critical Reception

Frankenstein received mixed reviews upon its publication, most appreciating the style of writing, but condemning the subject matter. The writer and critic Walter Scott wrote that 'upon the whole, the work impresses us with a high idea of the author's original genius and happy power of expression', but the *Quarterly Review* described it 'a tissue of horrible and disgusting absurdity'. Yet despite the reviews *Frankenstein* almost immediately became a popular success. A French translation appeared as early as 1821 (*Frankenstein: ou le Prométhée Moderne*, translated by Jules Saladin) and the novel's fame grew through melodramatic theatrical adaptations (in 1823 Mary Shelley saw a production of *Presumption; or The Fate of Frankenstein*, a play by Richard Brinsley Peake).

However, it would be some time before critics would look at Shelley's novel - or any Gothic novel - as a serious work of literature and initial critical attention often reduced *Frankenstein* to an aside to the work of her husband and the other Romantic poets. The first significant shift in critical reception occurred in the middle of the twentieth century when readers began to view the novel as an evocation of the modern condition: man trapped in a godless world in which science, ethics and morality have gone awry. Willingly, major twentieth century critics, like Harold Bloom, took it up with enthusiasm, exploring its Promethean and Miltonic echoes.

Other critics soon stressed the importance of bio-graphical criticism as a way of facilitating our understanding of the work, and such an approach has informed psychoanalytic and feminist criticism. The latter led a resurgence in Shelley criticism in the early 1980s, discovering within her work a source of rich commentary on gender roles and female experience at the beginning of the nineteenth century. However, at first the biographical emphasis tended to reduce Shelley's creative and intellectual achievement to an effect of postpartum depression, experienced when she lost one of her babies immediately after giving birth. Later critics explored more and more aspects of Shelley's familial relationships, often considering her novel as a reflection of complex oedipal conflicts, or finding in her an early and rich feminist voice.

Other writers and critics have considered its influence on popular culture. In his 1981 non-fiction book *Danse Macabre* author Stephen King considers the Creature to be an archetype of numerous horrific creations and views the novel as 'a Shakespearean tragedy'. He argues: 'its classical unity is broken only by the author's uncertainty as to where the fatal flaw lies - is it in Victor's hubris (usurping a power that belongs only to God) or in his failure to take responsibility for his creation after endowing it with the life-spark?'

Presumption: or the Fate of Frankenstein

Presumption: or the Fate of Frankenstein opened on 28 July 1823 and ran for 37 performances in London, with Mr T.P. Cooke a great success in the role of ——, as the play called Frankenstein's Creature. Mary Shelley attended a performance at the English Opera House on 29 August and wrote appreciatively to Leigh Hunt about Cooke's acting. Shelley liked 'this nameless mode of naming the unnameable' and she told Hunt that her father had brought out a new two-volume edition of the novel on the strength of the interest generated by

——

the dramatisation. Three more stage versions of *Frankenstein*, including the burlesque *Humgumption; or Dr Frankenstein and the Hobgoblin of Hoxton*, and *Presumption and the Blue Demon* appeared within the year and from 1823 to 1826 at least fifteen dramas employed characters and themes from Shelley's novel.

Studying the Gothic

When studying a Gothic text it is useful to consider certain key cultural and literary oppositions: barbarity versus civilisation; the wild versus the domestic (or domesticated); the supernatural versus the apparently 'natural'; that which lies beyond human understanding compared with that which we ordinarily encompass; the unconscious as opposed to the waking mind; passion versus reason; night versus day. Try applying these oppositions to *Frankenstein* and see where they take you in understanding the essential qualities of this genre.

It is also useful to make a distinction between 'terror' and 'horror': 'terror' is to be thought of as something more shadowy, more insubstantial, harder to pin down, as a suggestion or threat which builds over time; 'horror' stands for a gross physical shock, something which the reader can visualise. 'To awaken thrilling horror' was Mary Shelley's aim with *Frankenstein* (an aim, no doubt, which was more easily achieved with her contemporary reader than with today's). It is worth considering how we can define horror and terror today. It is also worth thinking about how they contribute to the central mood of the Gothic, which is fear. This mood generally has something to do with the past, with 'what comes back', with the revenant or the so-called undead. Usually the ghost that returns has some connection with an evil deed the protagonist has committed in the past, although occasionally there seems little clear reason for the 'return'. Freud identified the unconscious as that place in the mind from which nothing ever goes away and in the novel there is a clear connection with the past, the world of dreams and the unconscious mind. Moreover, guilty thoughts and illicit desires can surface, as with Victor Frankenstein's dream of his dead mother and Elizabeth.

Conventions and Elements of the Gothic

The novel which is thought to have started the Gothic tradition is Horace Walpole's *The Castle of Otranto* (1764). It became a popular genre in the late eighteenth century, and its conventions have been used by authors ever since. In the nineteenth century, parodies of the genre started appearing, because its conventions were so widely known. The conventions commonly found elements within Gothic novels include:

A plot which often involves a journey or pursuit.
Symbolism of light and dark.
A psychological element.
An introspective protagonist: brooding, lonely, uncertain, heroic status gained through struggle. Both Victor and the Creature are alienated individuals (see Romantic hero)
The creation of fear as a narrative priority.
Sinister and sublime settings – castles, ecclesiastical buildings, ruins, dungeons, secret passages, winding stairs, haunted buildings, dark and gloomy places, a wilderness, a graveyard, the inhospitable Arctic, rugged mountains, thick forests, generally bad weather.
Omens, ancestral curses and secrets.
Representation and stimulation of fear, horror and the macabre.
Tyrants, villains, maniacs, or simply focusing on the darkness of men's hearts, and other dark and bloody subjects.
Persecuted maidens, femme fatales, madwomen (think of first wives locked away in attics, incestuous sibling relationships, etc.).
Ghosts, monsters, demons, succubus, vampires.
Byronic heroes – intelligent, sophisticated and educated, but struggling with emotional conflicts, a troubled past and 'dark' attributes.

31

A combination of horror and romance; an appreciation of the joys of extreme emotion, the thrills of fearfulness and awe inherit in the sublime, and a quest for atmosphere.
Use of primitive, medieval, mysterious elements and horrifying, grotesque, supernatural events.
An atmosphere of degeneration and decay.

Early Gothic fiction was popular with female readers and thus explores themes relevant to the implied reader: the curious female (versus the solitary male on his quest for knowledge).

The Literary and Historical Context

Since the publication of Walpole's *The Castle of Otranto* Gothic literature has engendered a taste for the distasteful and an appetite for the pleasures of the flesh, although to the modern reader Walpole's giant helmets and speaking pictures now seem rather ridiculous. The works which were perceived in the late eighteenth century as most distinctively Gothic were those of Ann Radcliffe – chiefly *The Mysteries of Udolpho* and *The Italian* – and *The Monk* by Matthew Lewis. Mary Shelley's *Frankenstein*, though now usually seen as Gothic, appeared a little late in the period and was arguably more concerned with the perils of scientific experimentation than with the problems of ghosts and curses which preoccupied the Gothic. The second wave in the late nineteenth century was, perhaps, an accompaniment to *fin de siècle* notions of decadence and degeneration: Bram Stoker's *Dracula*, Robert Louis Stevenson's *The Strange Case of Dr Jekyll and Mr Hyde*, Wells's *The Island of Doctor Moreau* and Oscar Wilde's *The Picture of Dorian Gray*. Later, twentieth-century Gothic writing, from H.P. Lovecraft to Robert Bloch, has continued to test the limits of taste and horror and a penchant for the suburban Gothic has surfaced, particularly in film. Recently, with novels such as Susan Hill's *The Woman in Black* and Stephen Bywater's *Night of the Damned* we have the historical Gothic with settings either incorporating the motif of the haunted house or ranging far and wide with the latter set in the Amazon jungle in the 1930s.

However, to trace the Gothic back to its roots we have to consider the original Goths, who have been credited, at least in part, with the downfall of the Roman Empire and the sack of Rome. Sadly the Goths left almost no written records, and were mostly unheard of until the 'first Gothic revival' in the late eighteenth century. In Britain this revival involved a series of attempts to 'return to roots', in contrast to the classical model revered in the earlier eighteenth century. (Compare the neo-classical poetry of Alexander Pope to that of Wordsworth and you'll see a switch from the ornate and erudite to the relatively plain use of language and structure.)

The notion of the Gothic as a reaction against the neo-classical tradition had a considerable impact during the Romantic period, and influenced almost all the major Romantic writers in different ways. William Blake was an upholder of the Gothic as against the classical and Coleridge's ballad *The Rime of the Ancient Mariner* is arguably Gothic in its use of supernatural machinery. The earliest writers of the Gothic also made it clear that they were 'against reason' – they did not accept the classic Enlightenment view that humans are mainly driven by rational thought. On the contrary: the Gothic reminds us that we are mainly driven by our passions. This may be a good or a bad thing. It may be a good thing insofar as we might feel emotional intensity towards certain people or causes; it may be a bad thing insofar as it drives us into obsession or madness. At all events, the Gothic deals in illicit desires, in what is prohibited by society, in emotional extremes, whether terror or love, and terrifying forces.

Therefore Gothic texts can be seen as a reaction against the rational discourse that marked the literature and philosophy of The Age of Reason. Instead of Reason and Rationality the Imagination was set free; typified, some might argue, by Victor's overarching ambition. Gothic texts allowed readers to think the unthinkable; to sublimate their innermost desires within the pages of books that were in their very existence an affront to the intellectual establishment. As such they became a way of subverting the establishment. Novels that were concerned with outsiders and whose protagonists flouted the natural order became the obvious vehicle for attacking the safe, central values of a society that smugly turned its back on those who were not born into the comfort of money, education and power. The power and passion of Gothic literature seemed eminently suited to the iconoclasts, writers such as Lewis, Godwin, Shelley, who wished to challenge the status quo. Often the repressive regime is represented by an ancient order that resists change and any challenge to its autocratic rule. The heroes are those who seek to overturn this authority and establish the freedom to develop their individuality. In this sense the Gothic can echo the early ideals of the Romantic movement which sought to revolutionise society.

From this time on, the Gothic has continued to exert an influence. We can find it in the ghost story, which became extraordinarily popular during the Edwardian period when writers such as Arthur Conan Doyle and M.R. James wrote a number of distinctly Gothic tales. And we can find it in the more contemporary period with the evolution of the horror story in the hands of writers like those already mentioned and in the work of Angela Carter and Neil Gaiman. We can find it too in parodies of the Gothic such as Jane Austen's early nineteenth-century satire *Northanger Abbey*.

Gothic Language and Setting

The language in Gothic novels tends to be passionate, excessive, emotive; sensational and unrestrained by taste or moderation. The plot is often fantastical and the depiction of character – particularly in the early texts – is often crude. There is, according to some critics, little that is refined, rational or tasteful in the pages of these self-consciously lurid stories. Gothic texts tend to be about transgression, overstepping boundaries and entering a realm of the unknown. In this realm the ordinary is displaced by the extraordinary, the normal becomes the paranormal and the unconscious is as vivid, vital and valid as the conscious.

In this environment it becomes difficult to orientate one's self: it is often a dark world where winding passages lead deeper and deeper into an uncanny and uncertain world. Forests, wildernesses, extremes of nature predominate. The rational world is left far behind, reason no longer rules. The improbable is entirely possible and the impossible becomes ever more probable. Often the protagonist is presented with a baffling series of choices with no clear sense of what the right one might be and he or she has been removed – either by his or her own actions or by something beyond their control – from the old order of things.

The *ancien regime* (or old order) is frequently exemplified in old buildings: castles, abbeys, towers and so on. These features have become a sort of Gothic shorthand that signifies a past certainty or the dominance and barbarity of yesteryear. These buildings are often peopled by autocratic fathers, uncles, counts and kings.

Paradoxically, Gothic literature also lent itself to those who wished to warn society against the effects of breaking with the natural order: the protagonist, such as Victor, who strayed off the path of reason, order or decorum often came face-to-face with the consequences of their actions rendered all the more terrible in the lurid world of the Gothic text. Darkly attractive strangers who tempt the innocent and naïve are transformed into demonic villains who are only just defeated by some force of righteousness, even a personification of conventional morality, and the weeping victim is led back to safety a wiser and better person. The consequences of transgression are clearly delineated and the boundaries between order and chaos are endorsed and reinforced in the resurrection of an acceptable moral order (see Carter, Bywater).

In each Gothic text there is therefore a clearly defined threshold over which the protagonist and the reader must step. It may be represented as a physical boundary – the dividing line between the civilised and the natural world as in

Wuthering Heights. It might be a social line – the girl breaks free from the constraints of her family's expectations and rushes into the arms of some dubious stranger or it might be a moral line where the protagonist breaks a moral law – perhaps, like Victor, he has the temerity to imitate his Maker and breathe life into the inanimate.

Safe in the fictive world of Gothic literature the reader/viewer can vicariously experience the trials of those who have transgressed the boundaries of society, morality or sanity. They, unlike the protagonist, can overstep the margins of reasonable behaviour secure in the knowledge that they retain the power to shut the book, close the text and return to the rational world, albeit one which is all too familiar.

Gothic texts, in contrast, are traditionally set in foreign locations. At first these locations were literally exotic and far away – Italy, Spain, Arabia, Middle Europe but fairly quickly sublime landscapes closer to home were explored – Yorkshire, Scotland, Ireland, the Lake District. The fact that the 'foreign' could exist in the reader's own neighbourhood made it all the more frightening. In Jane Austen's *Northanger Abbey*, when the setting shifts from Bath to Northanger Abbey the description of the eponymous building is soon at odds with Catherine's expectations. Here, instead of the physical setting, the landscape of the mind becomes the ultimate other world where the self is lost in a welter of barely suppressed urges and desires. Often the viewer/reader is reading an externalised representation of his/her fascination with the unknowable and writers such as Mary Shelley and Jane Austen arguably anticipated the works of Freud in their exploration of the unconscious.

The Female Victim

At the heart of many Gothic texts is the tension provided by the possible violation of innocence – the concept of 'virtue in distress'. In the first flowering of the Gothic as a genre the innocent victim was almost exclusively female. Her chastity was the object of the villain's desire and the novel's landscapes and imagery often provided an obvious objective correlative for this sexual threat. Swords were raised, arrows let loose, doors forced and defences breached. Victims found themselves pursued down tortuous passages with no clear sight of an escape route: they were trapped in impossible situations and, as the genre developed, these were often of their own making. Sometimes their situation was made worse by the fact that their violation seemed to be legitimised by the laws of the land – the idea of the *droit du seigneur* Angela Carter memorably pastiches the latter in *The Bloody Chamber*.

In Gothic texts the preponderance of suffering women frequently foregrounds a struggle between the genders, a struggle in which men always have the upper hand. Texts such as *Jane Eyre*, of course, partially reverse this idea, since Jane, in a sense, 'wins'; but what she wins is an aged and blinded version of the man she loves. Certainly a great deal of Gothic fiction has been written by women, from Radcliffe through to Rice; and, much Gothic fiction seems to form itself around what psychologists might call 'eve-of-wedding fantasies' – those fantasies of lost freedom which women in particular have – or have had – before marriage (though ironically at the height of the Gothic, women had little freedom to lose!). There is a whole strand of criticism devoted to the 'female Gothic' – one of its main arguments hinges on the motif of the castle and its relation to the constrained domestic sphere which most women, in the late eighteenth and early nineteenth centuries, were forced to inhabit.

In *Frankenstein*, putting aside how human ambition might overstep the boundaries of creation, we also have a gender argument, since the protagonist also usurps the role of women in reproduction. It is also worth considering the novel from a biographical or even psychoanalytical perspective, informed by the fact that Mary Shelley's own mother died after giving birth to Mary. Indeed, some critics have seen the Creature's yearning for Victor as emblematic of Mary's own desire for her dead mother.

However, most if not all critics agree that the female characters in *Frankenstein,* with the possible exception of

Safie, typify the passive victim found in many early Gothic texts, unable to save themselves either from the feelings that they have or the situation they find themselves in.

Motifs

Temptation and transgression are the central motifs of the Gothic. The idea of forbidden fruit, the locked casket, room or house is the clichéd catalyst that still drives the majority of Gothic narratives. Either the protagonist actively oversteps the mark or he/she invites the danger into their own, previously safe environment; and it is curiosity that allows the reader to identify with the protagonist. At the heart of these stories of temptation there is a moral paradox. Surely, it can be argued, the pursuit of knowledge is a positive aspect of human endeavour – it is a fundamental aspect of the human condition and humanity refuses to be denied the answers to any question it might ask no matter how terrible the answer might be. Pushing the limits of knowledge and the consequences of such a search has become part and parcel of the scientific age and this has easily been assimilated into the Gothic model.

The forbidden knowledge or Faust motif takes its name from the German legend of Dr Faustus, who sold his soul to the devil to obtain power and knowledge forbidden to ordinary humans. Forbidden knowledge and power is often the Gothic protagonist's goal. The Gothic 'hero' questions the universe's ambiguous nature and tries to comprehend and control those supernatural powers that mortals cannot understand. He tries to overcome human limitations and make himself into a 'god'. This ambition usually leads to the hero's 'fall' or destruction; however, Gothic tales of ambition sometimes paradoxically evoke our admiration because they picture individuals with the courage to defy fate and cosmic forces in an attempt to transcend the mundane in order to achieve the eternal or sublime. It is also interesting to note that while men strive for knowledge and understanding, women are frequently portrayed as being merely curious.

The persecuted and frequently pursued maiden is another major motif as, of course, is the ghost. Ghosts have never been absent from literature – think, for example, of Shakespeare's *Hamlet* and *Richard III* – but in the Gothic we are constantly in the presence of ghosts, or at least of phenomena which might be considered ghostly, even if, as in the case of Radcliffe, they are usually explained away in the final few pages.

Other motifs include the Gothic castle, as in Dracula's castle and in works by Walpole, Radcliffe and Carter. The castle is a sinister, forbidding, a place where maidens find themselves persecuted by feudal barons, a reference to a medieval past which somehow remains as the site of our worst fears and terrors.

Then, of course, there is the vampire, who makes his first significant appearance in John Polidori's *The Vampyre* (1819) but becomes a source of obsession in much nineteenth-century literature. A particularly interesting example is the lesbian vampire in Sheridan Le Fanu's novella *Carmilla* (1871), although it is Stoker's *Dracula* (1897) who has most indelibly fixed himself in the minds of English readers.

Alongside these there are all manner of monsters (Mary Shelley's Creature is the most obvious), as well as the walking dead, which continue to surface in contemporary novels such as *Night of the Damned* (2015). A further, long-lived motif is the double, or doppelgänger, which is explored in *Frankenstein*, though *The Strange Case of Dr Jekyll and Mr Hyde* (1886) is the most obvious example.

Reading the Gothic

In France, the infamous Marquis de Sade wrote the first major criticism of the Gothic, attributing its growth to the dangers and terrors of the French Revolution (which some critics see the Creature in *Frankenstein* as symbolizing). Some argue that the Gothic is a response to anxieties that the ancient feudal, aristocratic order might return to unsettle bourgeois conventions, a set of conventions which, on the surface, seemed certain of dominance during the eighteenth century but which were, perhaps, not quite as secure as they seemed. Aristocrats are frequently vilified, yet there is also the fear of the mob.

In Gothic novels the normal world is rendered void and the reader becomes complicit in whatever he or she might encounter. The vicarious thrill lies in shared act of transgression – the reader is tasting forbidden fruit, opening dangerous boxes in the hope of enjoying the illicit pleasures made available to the protagonist. The narrative often involves journeys into the unknown and this is a metaphorical enactment of the act of 'reading' text itself. The texts themselves are often forbidden; beyond the bounds of acceptable literature and the very act of reading them is, in itself, a flouting of the authority of the legitimate canon of 'worthy texts'. Perhaps it is the darkness within us, the desire for bloodshed or the taboo, which craves what these damned and damning texts contain.

Key Quotations

In what is referred to as a 'closed book' exam you will be required to learn quotations in order to illustrate your point or opinion. A quotation can be a single word, a short phrase or a line or two. Examiners will not expect you to quote several lines and to do so, at least without a close critical analysis of each line, is likely to be counterproductive. Below are lines taken from the novel which give you the opportunity to focus on key ideas within the text.

To awaken thrilling horror (Mary Shelley)

Divine wanderer (Walton describing Victor)

My more than sister (Victor)

A new species would bless me as its creator and source (Victor)

No father could claim the gratitude of his child so completely as I should deserve theirs (Victor)

I pursued nature to her hiding place (Victor)

It was on a dreary night in November (Victor)

Men appear to me as monsters (Elizabeth)

William and Justine … the first hapless victims of my unhallowed arts (Victor)

I ought to be thy Adam; but I am rather the fallen angel (Creature)

Misery made me a fiend (Creature)

I am malicious because I am miserable (Creature)

I am a blasted tree (Victor)

Make me happy again and I shall again be virtuous (Creature)

I will be with you on your wedding night (Creature)

Destiny was too potent, and her immutable laws had decreed my utter and terrible destruction (Victor)

…avoid ambition… yet another may succeed (Victor to Walton)

Key Passages

When reading the following passages you should consider how you would describe the narrative voice. Does it shift within the extract? Whose point of view is being given? Which character is the focaliser, if any? What words or phrases or aspects of the extract helped you decide? What's the effect of the narrative voice in each case?

After you have read the extract, and made your own notes, read the critical response below. Does it give you any fresh knowledge/information that's useful in reading the novel? Does it confirm your interpretation of the novel or help to develop your own understanding? If it challenges your own interpretation of the novel consider why.

After reading the critical response you are advised to highlight one or two short phrases which you might use in an essay to develop your argument or viewpoint. You could then go on to write a paragraph in which you incorporate the quotation and your own thoughts.

Extract 1

St. Petersburgh, Dec. 11th, 17 –

TO Mrs. Saville, England

You will rejoice to hear that no disaster has accompanied the commencement of an enterprise which you have regarded with such evil forebodings. I arrived here yesterday, and my first task is to assure my dear sister of my welfare and increasing confidence in the success of my undertaking. I am already far north of London, and as I walk in the streets of Petersburgh, I feel a cold northern breeze play upon my cheeks, which braces my nerves and fills me with delight. Do you understand this feeling? This breeze, which has travelled from the regions towards which I am advancing, gives me a foretaste of those icy climes.

Critical Response

Mary Shelley begins the novel with the letters from Walton to his sister, the passive and ideal reader, Mrs Margaret Saville, and it quickly becomes apparent that Walton is engaged in a very Victor-like project. He too wants to break

---

42

through boundaries and pursue his dreams, even if they take him deep into the uncharted Polar wastes. At the end of the fourth letter Mary Shelley cleverly suspends the explorer's narrative while Walton finds himself compelled to listen to Victor's story. And while that narrative is being shared we know there is a huge amount hanging on its reception by Walton who becomes an author-cum-copyist.

Walton keeps writing, as he moves from letters to a letter journal. But Victor Frankenstein intrudes and Walton's journal becomes Victor's confessional autobiography. When the Creature subsequently invades his creator's narrative, civilized and formal authority gives way to an eloquent and impassioned response. Finally, when Walton resumes his letters, he abandons the formalities of dating and address and we read no proper valediction or closing signature.

Extract 2

It was on a dreary night of November that I beheld the accomplishment of my toils. With an anxiety that almost amounted to agony, I collected the instruments of life around me, that I might infuse a spark of being into the lifeless thing that lay at my feet. It was already one in the morning; the rain pattered dismally against the panes, and my candle was nearly burnt out, when, by the glimmer of the half-extinguished light, I saw the dull yellow eye of the Creature open; it breathed hard, and a convulsive motion agitated its limbs.

How can I describe my emotions at this catastrophe, or how delineate the wretch whom with such infinite pains and care I had endeavoured to form?

Critical Response

The above extract incorporates a Gothic lexis with the use of words such as 'dreary', 'November' and 'lifeless'. The adjective 'dreary' is fitting for the melancholy and dismal setting, the month of November signifies the end of the year and conveys the idea of death and inclement weather. That the

'Rain pattered dismally against the panes' can be viewed as pathetic fallacy, even nature can be seen to be crying for the death of the mother which Victor's unnatural creation represents. The 'half-extinguished light' gives the reader the Gothic half-light we would expect for the culmination of Victor's 'unhallowed arts'. The dull yellow eye opening gives the Creature a rather sinister almost reptilian appearance, and the fact that only one eye opens is also rather disturbing. The 'Creature' then quickly becomes a 'catastrophe' and then a 'wretch', with Victor in the final interrogative sentence focusing on his own sorry feelings rather than the Creature's disorientation.

Exam Questions

'Man,' I cried, 'how ignorant art thou in thy pride of wisdom!' Discuss the theme of the use and misuse of knowledge in the novel.

Mary Shelley wanted to write a novel that 'would speak to the mysterious fears of our nature.' How successful is she in creating fear and suspense in *Frankenstein*?

Who, in your view, is the victim in *Frankenstein,* and why?

How far do you think that *Frankenstein* represents a criticism of society?

How far do you agree with the view that the real villain of the novel is not the Creature but Victor Frankenstein himself?

How far, for you, is the Creature successful in presenting a rational explanation for his actions?

To what extent do you agree that in her portrayal of the monster and his story, 'Mary Shelley demonstrates the corruption of an innocent Creature by an immoral society'?

In her Introduction to the 1831 edition of *Frankenstein,* Mary Shelley wrote that she hoped her story 'would speak to the mysterious fears of our nature and awaken thrilling horror...' By what means, and to what extent, do you think she succeeded?

The novel's sub-title – *The Modern Prometheus* – has been said to shed much light on Mary Shelley's key themes in *Frankenstein.* To what extent do you agree with this view and why?

'Although clearly a remarkable and spirited young woman herself, Mary Shelley created in *Frankenstein* a series of passive and uninteresting female characters.' What is your view of the presentation and function of the female characters in the novel?

'Far from making him the Romantic hero he would like to appear to be, Mary Shelley presents Victor Frankenstein as the villain of his own story.' To what extent do you accept this view of Mary Shelley's approach towards her central character?

Within Gothic literature the female characters are often portrayed as passive victims. Some are even conveyed as consciously submissive, others become victims because of their uncontrollable curiosity. Discuss this view in relation to *Frankenstein.*

By the end of the novel does Mary Shelley want the reader to feel more sympathy for Victor or the Creature?

While considering the Gothic genre and its generic feature, how satisfying is the end of Frankenstein?

Many critics have commented that the Creature is ultimately a character with whom we sympathise. Explore Shelley's presentation of the Creature in the light of this comment.

Essay Question and Model Answer

To what extent do you agree with the view that Victor in *Frankenstein* is more monstrous than the Monster?

In *Frankenstein* there are numerous examples of monstrosity, such as Victor's construction of the Creature where he 'disturbed the human frame' and collected bones from churchyards and charnel houses. This is both gruesome and sacrilegious, reminiscent of the church-offending grave robbers and pitiless scientists of the Victorian era, and yet typical of Gothic literature. There are also other instances which are monstrous, such as Felix De Lacey's vicious rejection of the Creature based on his appearance, though some might argue that it was a justified response to an eight-foot tall, physically intimidating being described as 'too horrible for human eyes'. However, the degree of monstrosity differs when we consider the alternative perspective. For example, Felix attacking a figure who clung beseechingly to his blind father's knees.

Yet to answer the question we must first ask ourselves does 'monstrosity' lie within Victor or in the Creature? Victor's creation is of such an 'unearthly ugliness' - a 'filthy mass' born in a 'workshop of filthy creation' - that even Walton, who has heard his story, cannot ignore the 'appalling hideousness'. Superficially the character fulfils our expectations of a monster, but we cannot label him thus. Shelley shows that all the aspects which repel other characters are the ones crafted by Victor's hand: it was not the Creature who dragged the dead body parts from the graves nor committed ungodly acts sullying the purity of creation. Everything about the Creature that Victor could control, his appearance and his birth, are monstrous, and everything he cannot, which is the mind, is initially unprejudiced, open-minded and intelligent. Yet even when Victor recognises the 'wickedness' of his deeds, and though his 'heart often sickened' at the 'work of my hands', he does nothing to remedy the situation. His passion for success overrides his

---

46

ability to make a moral choice to such an extent that, for the contemporary reader, he commits the *most* horrific violation of nature by trying to imitate God. This, in the early nineteenth century, is arguably far more monstrous than the arson, murder and violence committed by the Creature, one who becomes emblematic of the French Revolution (originally full of noble intentions, yet descending into bloodshed).

The Creature didn't set out to act monstrously but, as he suffered no 'reward for my benevolence' but simply rejection, he felt forced to take action. Conversely, Victor and other characters in the novel cannot justify by discrimination their subsequent cruelty to the Creature: William rejects the Creature because he has been taught to judge ugliness by society or has inherited the innate prejudice which humans have, whereas the Creature, not quite human, does not begin with this quality.

Moreover, Victor not only creates this 'odious and loathsome' being but then abandons it. He needlessly crafts something physically unfit for the world with the desire to be worshipped by creatures who 'owe their being' to him, and then, upon seeing the reality of his 'darkness', he flees and takes no responsibility. This is perhaps the most unnatural part of the entire novel as we expect him to care for his offspring. After all he imitates the process of 'painful labour' and creation, eliminating the mother role, and then fails to fulfil his responsibilities as a parent. Perhaps the Creature allows Victor to escape from his repressed inclinations, a doppelganger for himself which he is unwilling to nurture. Perhaps he wants to engineer something doomed to suffer because of its appearance, punishing it with a lack of mother as he himself is deprived of his mother or perhaps it has something to do with his engagement to Elizabeth. He notes that the female Creature might 'refuse to comply with a compact made before her Creation' possibly alluding to his own resentment for being bound to marry his 'more than sister'. Does he unconsciously feel trapped in a semi-incestuous relationship which he shows little passion for within the text. This may be why he destroys the female Creature and breaks his promise, something which he cannot do with Elizabeth.

Furthermore, not only does he eliminate the mother role, but he has incestuous dreams about kissing his mother 'crawling with grave worms' and clearly has some aversion to the sexual act. He abandons his wife on his wedding night having created a being which he denies a mate. Victor manipulates the laws of life and death to comfort his own turmoil of emotion, which is heartless, selfish and monstrous. The Creature is not a monster; he is a *victim* of Victor's repressed monstrosity.

Of course the etymology of 'monster' suggests something to be looked at and the Creature with his 'conglomeration of ill-matching parts' fits this particular description perfectly (see *Ideas on the Monstrous* by Peter Brooks). Other characters in the novel are described as 'angelic', 'pretty', 'exquisitely beautiful' and 'cherub'-like, and in a binary opposition their appearance is natural and un-monstrous. By this the Creature is 'more monstrous' than the humans. Yet it is difficult to judge many of the characters we meet by anything other than their appearance or demeanour. For example, it is difficult to judge the women in the novel on their behaviour because they are generally passive or reticent. Justine is referred to as 'tranquil', 'frank-hearted' and 'gentle' of which there is nothing vaguely repellent. Only Safie, who has gleaned the masculine characteristics of self-preservation and shed something of the others' femininity can be described as having a will of her own. Indeed the most passive of characters is surely Walton's sister, the silent reader.

Allied to her brother's noble ambition this merely serves to highlight the monstrosity of Victor by foregrounding the ruthlessness of his own actions in relation to the actions of others. And for the reader the Creature's narrative changes everything: it illuminates the consequences of Victor's inhumanity by demonstrating the suffering of his creation, and draws our attention to his subjective portrayal of the Creature as a two-dimensional, bloodthirsty fiend of 'unparalleled barbarity'. Moreover, when we meet the Creature he is eloquent, greeting him with 'I expected this reception'.

Shelley, one could argue, is showing Victor did this to disguise or justify his own internal monstrosity, and to lessen the horror of his own abandonment of his Creature. What he cast aside was fully formed, intelligent and instinctively moral. Victor has therefore lost more than his loved ones by acting heartlessly and impulsively: he has arguably lost his soul and, perhaps most monstrous of all, has forfeited the Creature's own potential for goodness.

PART TWO – REVISION NOTES

The following revision notes are written in note form and will help you to focus on the key terms and ideas before an exam.

Critical Vocabulary

Eponymous male protagonist; VF; epistolary; verisimilitude; filter – Walton filters all of the novel, Victor also gives a subjective account of the Creature; embedded narrative – Creature's, Victor's narrative is also embedded in Walton's letters that act as a *framing device*; unreliable first person narrator(s); autodiegetic narrator is the protagonist in the novel (victor becomes the autodiegetic narrator, homodiegetic – narrator who is character in the novel, shifting narratives; denouement; formal archaisms – used by Creature; paradox; oxymoron; juxtaposition; religious lexis – 'serpent', 'thy lover is near'; symbolism/symbolise/symbolic; binary oppositions; doppelgänger/alter-ego; embodiment – Creature is embodiment of Victor's repressed desires/ base instincts; transgression/subversion; intertextuality.

Form and Structure

Epistolary form gives verisimilitude, a popular albeit a rather archaic method of authorship; form as a confession (with Walton as confessor); Andrew McCulloch: 'Walton is an ironic pre-echo of Victor'; Shelley uses three male narrators to tell the story, even when is revolves around woman, suggesting that women's lives are narrated, or even dictated, by men; embedding of the Creature's narrative means the reader is prejudiced against him by Victor's previous narration (and Walton's evident sympathy and admiration for him); echoes human experience as children are socialised to associate physical deformity with internal monstrosity, as William proves, disappointing Creature who hopes he 'had lived too short a time to have imbibed a horror of deformity'.

Creature and Victor are recounting their tales for a specifically stated purpose (to persuade their listener), which raises additional questions about their reliability; Chinese box structure confines the anarchic and subversive rebellions of the characters; incestuous dream comes after animation of motherless creature – death of the mother is thus highlighted by Shelley; significance of William's murder: Creature becomes a murderer or destroyer and therefore reader begins to question the extent to which Victor can reasonably be held accountable for his actions; point at which the threat of the Creature, perceived by Victor from his animation, moves from psychological fear of an unrealised threat (terror) to the physical damage of a threat carried out (horror); end of belief in the power of the 'god-like science' of language to save him from eternal isolation; structural significance of the fact that Victor's destruction of the Creature's mate precedes the Creature's murder of Elizabeth – the parallel links the two characters as inextricably linked doubles, but the Creature's emulation of Victor does not make him any more (or less) evil than Victor.

Novel's lack of closure and failure to complete epistolary form leaves reader with a sense of unease, compounded by the lack of proof that the Creature has killed himself, he is thus imbued with a symbolic resonance as the ongoing threat of scientific endeavour/human (over) achievement.

Use of Language

Binary oppositions – creator/Creature ('a new species would bless me as their creator and source'/'thy Adam') – father/ son ('an abortion'); pejorative words/phrases used by Victor – 'ghastly grin', 'demon', 'fiend', 'wretch' and 'monster'; William cries 'hideous monster' which echoes Victor's language, thus suggesting inevitability/universality of the response; Walton refers to Victor as the Creature's 'prey' and 'victim', an echo of Victor's misunderstanding of Creature's reaching hand; 'I like the arch-fiend... bore a hell within me' – same phrase used by Victor and Creature.

The word 'ardour' used by all three narrators (by Walton and Victor in relation to learning, Creature in relation to virtue – almost sexual word for intellectual passion – lack of physical/emotional intimacy (especially of Victor); 'workshop of filthy creation' uses oxymoron to demonstrate how he has made pure act 'filthy' by using science to sully nature – use of dead body parts – exclusion of the female; 'the tempest, so beautiful yet terrific', link to Shakespeare's *The Tempest* (Caliban with Creature).

'Budding with fresh spring... not knowing exactly what path to pursue' Creature's description of setting (crossroads) just before saves girl and is shot – 'fresh spring' could be his recent happiness, which the encounter ruins, and 'path'/crossroads could be a moral decision as this marks a turning point in his life ('I vowed eternal hatred and vengeance on all mankind')

'My heart swelled with exaltation and hellish triumph' – Creature understands that killing William is morally wrong or even evil, denoted by the word 'hellish', yet still commits the action and takes pleasure from having done so – yet his understanding of morals here (making him immoral not amoral) shows him to be advanced beyond the brutish animal William sees.

Creature uses formal archaisms such as 'thy Adam' – shows his eloquence to be equal, if not superior, to that of other narrators; Creature often connects the word 'vice' to humans – 'so vicious and base', 'vice and bloodshed', 'the vices of mankind' – suggesting he views humans as immoral and flawed, contrasting with his (self-described) morality 'ardour for virtue... abhorrence for vice'.

'My vices are the children of a forced solitude' – novel can be seen as birth myth therefore 'children' is eye-catching – endorses William Godwin's views on isolation as root of evil – also Creature's isolation is 'forced' whereas Victor's is willing; Creature speaks in complex sentences in contrast to Victor's, which are fractured by punctuation – 'Begone, vile insect! or, rather, stay, that I may trample you to dust!'

Creature says of Justine 'the crime had its source in her: be hers the punishment!' – links Justine to Eve (and original sin), a common justification for patriarchal control as women were believed to be susceptible to temptation; Creature refers to Safie as if her father 'possessed a treasure' to 'reward' Felix with – she is objectified and the implication is that she can be both owned and traded for the benefit of men; women constantly equated with angelic language in narration of both Victor and Creature, which makes them 'other' from the male protagonists – they are idealised whereas female creature (with potential for free will and possible ugliness) is demonised.

Victor's father 'conducted [Caroline] to Geneva, placed her under the protection of a relative' – Caroline is an object in both phrases and passively allows herself to be controlled; 'insensible to the charms of nature' while creating Creature – possibly suggestion of lack of attraction to woman (Elizabeth) as the 'charms of nature' which he is insensible to, as suggested by Elizabeth's death before he can consummate marriage; in Victor's dream, Elizabeth is 'in the bloom of health' which is possibly a reference to pregnancy, inclusion of dream as this point could be highlighting the fact that he could have made a son in the natural way; Elizabeth's corpse is 'flung by the murderer on its bridal bier'.

Victor's willing isolation of himself in the Orkneys suggests he is punishing himself as a way to expiate his guilt: 'all of the squalidness of the most miserable penury'; Female creature 'might refuse to comply with a compact made before her creation' which explicitly refers to the Creature's promise to 'quit the neighbourhood of man' upon delivery of his mate, but could also be the implicit social and cultural agreement that women are subservient and inferior to men – destruction of female creature is both Victor's fear of a woman with free will, and his fear that if she rejects both the Creature and human society, she would not be taught patriarchal values.

Victor and Elizabeth 'walked for a short time on the shore', later Creature 'plunged into the lake' – Victor observes nature whereas Creature literally jumps in as he is closer to

53

nature.

To Walton: 'gratification of your wishes may not be a serpent to sting you, as mine has been' – Victor externalises ambition as poison/curse that corrupts from outside (using religious symbolism), rather than an internal characteristic.

Creature's talk with Walton uses repeated reversals, typical of Gothic binary oppositions, saying 'virtue has become to me a shadow' and 'happiness and affection are turned into bitter and loathing despair' – pairings reflect his descent from innocence and pure spirit into the monstrous.

'I too can create desolation' is an oxymoronic statement, with the 'too' denoting that the 'creation of desolation' is a human skill which he is emulating.

Gothic and Literary Context

Gothic tradition of 'discovered' stories (gives verisimilitude) such as *Castle of Otranto* – later copied by *Dracula, Wuthering Heights*; becomes a literary trope or cliché and starts science-fiction genre while simultaneously reviving Gothic which had become predictable, leading to Gothic parodies such as Austen's *Northanger Abbey* (published the same year as the original version of *Frankenstein*, 1818).

Walton says Arctic is 'the seat of frost and desolation' (see Dante's *Inferno*, the 9th circle of hell is reserved for people who betray their family and friends) therefore Victor's death here is symbolic of his crime. *The Nightmare* painting (1781) by Fuseli – similar to 'body flung by the murderer on its bridal bier' – gives sexual connotation to description.

Victor calls Clerval 'the very poetry of nature', a quote from the Romantic poem *The Story of Rimini* by Leigh Hunt – this is in the Rhine where Victor is Gothic and Clerval Romantic; extreme ambition (also tragic) and lack of emotional sensitivity/care are traditionally male characteristics within the Gothic – Victor embodies this, while Clerval opposes it; Agatha faints at the sight of the Creature, as a typical weak Gothic heroine would; doppelgänger/alter-ego – 'my own spirit let loose from the grave'.

Social Context

William Godwin (Mary's father) believed isolation caused humanity's problems and should be avoided, also believed in perfectibility through education and questions authority; there is no useful authority in novel (no God, human authorities unjust to Safie, De Laceys and Justine).

Mary Wollstonecraft (Mary's mother) was an early feminist – women are oppressed by men, although fail to escape patriarchal oppression and control – possible criticism as Safie's empowerment leads her to take on negative male characteristics (callousness) as she abandons Agatha; patriarchal society: women could only exist in the domestic sphere, thus Elizabeth's 'simple and powerful' defence of Justine in court is fruitless, and both women are killed outside their domestic setting – Justine dies because Victor fails to defend her, choosing the maintenance of his own reputation over her life – Elizabeth, Safie and female creature are all used in a transaction (albeit Elizabeth's is by a woman – internalised patriarchal values).

Prometheus was admired by Romantics as an ambitious character striving to better human condition; *Paradise Lost* – Creature links with Adam and Satan; Victor links with God, Adam/Eve and Satan.

Geneva – birthplace of Protestantism (radical and also strong connection to England; move away from Gothic tradition of Catholic settings which makes setting less alien/other to British readers); Ingolstadt – birthplace of C18 Illuminati (Enlightenment) who were supposedly connected to French Revolution – full of Gothic architecture which is not mentioned in novel; French Revolution – Creature starts with noble aims but is corrupted by circumstance; Reign of Terror killed innocents because of family connections (William).

In the early 19th century there was a commonly held belief that external beauty or deformity reflected internal beauty or deformity – Creature says 'I became fully convinced that I was in reality the monster that I am' – women are all beautiful, Victor is 'attractive and amiable' according to

Walton; Creature is 'hideous' – only blind De Lacey is kind to Creature.

Contemporary society attached importance to religious morality/purity which makes Victor's dream even more disturbing/shocking/transgressive than it is to a modern reader; contemporary Christian teachings make Victor's desire to 'have a new race bless of beings... bless me as their creator and source' was blasphemous as he is seeking to usurp God's position as only God can create life – to a modern readership the father abandoning the son leads to a harsher condemnation. A modern audience can read the novel with an awareness of the Oedipus complex: Victor's dream with its incestuous implications and the Creature seeking to destroy his 'father'.

Literary Criticism and Interpretations

Shelley hoped to 'speak to the mysterious fears of our nature and awaken thrilling horror' – 'let my hideous progeny go forth and prosper' which it has, spawning countless film and theatre adaptations. Peter Brooks on the Creature: 'as a verbal creation he is the very opposite of the monstrous'; Jane Bathard-Smith: Creature is physically 'a vile conglomeration of ill-matching parts' – Victor is 'a manipulating intermediary, perhaps anxious to justify his own internal monstrosity'; Andrew McCulloch: Creature is 'a walking compendium of broken taboos and illicit aspirations' – 'seemingly asexual 'production' of Elizabeth' leads to Victor's unhealthy view of women and parenting – Walton is an 'ironic pre-echo of Victor'; Anne Mellor: 'cultural encoding of the female as passive and possessable, the willing receptacle of male desire' – women gained power within household by having family and running domestic space but Elizabeth is denied both these duties by Victor – women are confined to domestic sphere and excluded from intellectual settings of university, therefore 'intellectual activity is segregated from emotional activity' so Victor cannot love his friends/family while constructing the Creature, and cannot engage emotionally with him.

Freudian reading: Creature is id and Victor's dream is

suggestive of latent 'incestuous' desires; also destruction of the father by the Creature fits the Oedipus complex.

Marxist reading: Creature is the proletariat (the working class); ties in with idea of him being embodiment of French Revolution.

Revision Topics

The wider revision topics below are worth considering, though it is important to find out what your exam board expects by way of assessment objectives; e.g. is context to be rewarded? The revision topics can also be treated as research topics for presentations.

Mary Shelley
The Romantic Movement
The Gothic Genre
Frankenstein in Popular Culture
Frankenstein and its Critical Reception
Prometheus
Milton and Goethe
Paracelsus and Agrippa
Mary Wollstonecraft
William Godwin
The Epistolary Novel
Scientific Knowledge in the Early 19th Century

Glossary

Bildungsroman: a formation novel or coming-of-age story; a literary genre that focuses on the psychological and moral growth of the protagonist from youth to adulthood and in which character development is thus extremely important.

Byronic: Byron appears to embody wild and seductive masculinity and it is because he is so romantically aloof, that fictional literary characters with similar enigmatic and impressive qualities have been called 'Byronic'. Heathcliff in

Emily Brontë's *Wuthering Heights* and Victor Frankenstein in Mary Shelley's *Frankenstein* have been so-called for their resemblance to the notorious nineteenth-century aristocrat.

Like Byron, Frankenstein is from a 'most distinguished' family, has money, friends and property, the social instruments which his monster laments being deprived of. Yet Frankenstein throws away his advantages in pursuit of 'glory and 'self-satisfaction'.

Doppelgänger: (literally double-goer) a look-alike or double of a living person. In *Frankenstein* Victor and the Creature have a symbiotic relationship at the end of the novel with the latter arguably representing Victor's dark nature.

Epistolary: an epistolary novel is written as a series of documents. The usual form is letters although diary entries, newspaper clippings and other documents are sometimes used. The epistolary form can add greater realism or verisimilitude to a story, because it mimics the workings of real life. It is thus able to demonstrate differing points of view without recourse to the device of an omniscient narrator. There are three types of epistolary novels: monologic (giving the letters of only one character, like Letters of a Portuguese Nun), dialogic (giving the letters of two characters), and polylogic (with three or more letter-writing characters, such as in Bram Stoker's *Dracula*). In addition, a crucial element in polylogic epistolary novels like *Clarissa*, and *Dangerous Liaisons* is the dramatic device of 'discrepant awareness': the simultaneous but separate correspondences of the heroines and the villains creating dramatic tension.

Eponymous: (adjective) of, relating to, or being the person or entity after which something or someone is named. Frankenstein is the eponymous protagonist or 'hero' of the novel; Northanger Abbey is the eponymous setting for Jane Austen's novel.

Free indirect discourse or speech: is a third person narrative which uses some of the characteristics of third-person along with the essence of first person direct speech. What distinguishes free indirect discourse or speech from normal indirect speech is the lack of an introductory expression such as 'She said' or 'She thought'. It is as if the subordinate clause carrying the content of the indirect speech is taken out of the main clause. Using free indirect speech may convey the character's words more directly than in normal indirect, as devices such as interjections and exclamation marks can be used that cannot be normally used within a subordinate clause. Jane Austen is cited as one of the first novelists to use this style consistently. Quoted or direct speech: He laid down his bundle and thought of his misfortune. 'And just what pleasure have I found, since I came into this world?' he asked. Reported or normal indirect speech: He laid down his bundle and thought of his misfortune. He asked himself what pleasure he had found since he came into the world. Free indirect speech: He laid down his bundle and thought of his misfortune. And just what pleasure had he found, since he came into this world?

Motif: any recurring element that has symbolic significance in a story. Through its repetition, a motif can help produce other narrative (or literary) aspects such as theme or mood. While it may appear interchangeable with the related concept theme the term 'motif' does differ somewhat in usage. Any number of narrative elements with symbolic significance can be classified as motifs - whether they are images, spoken or written phrases, structural or stylistic devices, or other elements like sound, physical movement, or visual components in dramatic narratives. To distinguish between a motif and theme a general rule is that a theme is abstract and a motif is concrete.

Narrator: it is worth considering the different types beyond the first person (the 'I' in a story). A narrator who is also a character in the story is a homodiegetic narrator. If the homodiegetic narrator is also the protagonist of the narrative, it is an autodiegetic narrator.

Radcliffean: in *The Radcliffean Gothic Model: A Form for Feminine Sexuality* Cynthia Wolff addresses sexuality in Gothic novels and how women have to deal with the 'virgin/whore' syndrome. It is also interesting to note that while women fall into the category of virgin/whore, men fall into the category of villains and/or heroes. Wolff writes, 'The heroine becomes 'somebody' when she is united with such a man. Marriage seals the bargain by which she becomes mistress of the castle.' Within *Frankenstein* Elizabeth can be seen as the passive Radcliffean heroine.

Romantic hero: is a literary archetype referring to a character that rejects established norms and conventions, has been rejected by society, and has the self as the centre of his or her own existence. The Romantic hero is often the protagonist in the literary work and there is a primary focus on the character's thoughts rather than his or her actions. Literary critic Northrop Frye noted that the Romantic hero is often 'placed outside the structure of civilization and therefore represents the force of physical nature, amoral or ruthless, yet with a sense of power, and often leadership, that society has impoverished itself by rejecting'. Other characteristics of the romantic hero include introspection, the triumph of the individual over the 'restraints of theological and social conventions', wanderlust, melancholy, and isolation. Another common trait of the Romantic hero is regret for his actions.

Southern Gothic: combines some Gothic sensibilities (such as the grotesque) with the setting and style of the Southern United States. Examples include William Faulkner and Poppy Z Brite.

Suburban Gothic: a subgenre of Gothic fiction, film and television, focused on anxieties associated with the creation of suburban communities, particularly in the United States, from the 1950s and 1960s onwards. It often, but not exclusively, relies on the supernatural but manifested in a suburban setting; an early example being Ira Levin's *Rosemary's Baby*.

A List of Gothic Novels and Short Stories

Frankenstein – Mary Shelley, 1818
Northanger Abbey – Jane Austen, 1818
The Tell-Tale Heart – Edgar Allan Poe, 1843
Jane Eyre - Charlotte Brontë, 1847
Wuthering Heights – Emily Brontë, 1847
The Mystery of Edwin Drood – Charles Dickens, 1870
The Strange Case of Dr Jekyll and Mr Hyde – Robert Louis Stevenson, 1886
The Beetle – Richard Marsh, 1897
Dracula – Bram Stoker, 1897
The Rats in the Walls – H.P. Lovecraft, 1923
Rebecca – Daphne du Maurier, 1938
Rosemary's Baby – Ira Levin, 1967
The Shining – Stephen King, 1977
The Bloody Chamber – 1977, Angela Carter
Interview with a Vampire – Anne Rice, 1977
Bellefleur – Joyce Carol Oates, 1980
Lost Souls – Poppy Z Brite, 1992
House of Leaves – Mark Z Danielewski, 2000
Frankenstein in Baghdad – Ahmed Saadawi, 2010
Floating Staircase – Ronald Malfi, 2011
Night of the Damned – Stephen Bywater, 2015

Further Critical Reading

Gothic Horror: A Critical Anthology - Clive Bloom
Gothic, the New Critical Idiom - Fred Botting
Nightmare: Birth of Horror - Christopher Frayling
Love, Mystery and Misery: Feeling in Gothic Fiction - Coral Ann Howells
The Radcliffean Gothic Model: A Form of Feminine Sexuality - Modern Language Studies - Cynthia Griffin Wolff
The Literature of Terror: A History of Gothic Fiction from 1765 to the Present Day - David Punter
Frankenstein, Penguin Critical Studies - Maurice Hindle
Frankenstein, York Notes Advanced - Glennis Byron

Mary Shelley, a Critical Biography - Muriel Spark
The Madwoman in the Attic - Sandra M. Gilbert and Susan
Gubar
Frankenstein, Macmillan New Casebook - edited by Fred
Botting

Mary Shelley – A Short Biography

William Godwin, Mary's father, was a prominent political theorist who encouraged her to read widely. Among the books she would have known well would have been his own novel *Caleb Williams* (1794). It contains elements of the Gothic but it is the psychological struggle it depicts between a young man and his aristocratic enemy that is of greater importance to Frankenstein, prefiguring the opposition between Victor and the Creature. *Caleb Williams* also shares the pace of Godwin's other novels and the journeying and pursuit is there in *Frankenstein*.

Both Godwin and Mary's mother, Mary Wollstonecraft, had a very strong sense of the importance of education and of the power of literature to have a transforming impact on society. They believed that the dissemination of ideas, discussion and debate have an essential role to play in humankind's progression. (the next chapter contains a more detailed account of her parents).

Mary's childhood was relatively happy, though after meeting Shelley her life soon became blighted by tragedy. Between 1815 and 1819 she lost three of the four children. It is also worth noting that the period of Walton's letters to his sister is nine months and that the first victim of the Creature, the child William, shared the name of Mary's son who was still alive in 1816 when the story was first conceived.

In 1822 her husband drowned when his sailing boat sank during a storm. A year later, Mary Shelley returned to England and from then on devoted herself to the upbringing of her only surviving child, Percy Florence Shelley, and to her career as a professional author. The last decade of her life was dogged by illness, probably caused by the brain tumour that was to kill her in 1851 at the age of 53.

Mrs Shelley by Lucy Maddox Rossetti (Publ.1890)

The following excerpts taken from *Mrs Shelley* shed further light on Mary Shelley's life and include a near-contemporary summary of the novel.

Mary Wollstonecraft, one of the most remarkable and misunderstood women of even her remarkable day, was born in April 1759. Her father, son of a Spitalfields manufacturer, possessed an adequate fortune for his position; her mother was of Irish family. They had six children, of whom Mary was the second. Mary Wollstonecraft's scheme in the *Vindication of the Rights of Woman* is, according to Lucy Madox Rossetti, summed up below:

> She wished women to have education equal to that of men.
> That trades, professions, and other pursuits should be open to women.
> That married women should own their own property as in other European countries.
> That they should have more facilities for divorce from husbands guilty of immoral conduct.
> That, in the case of separation, the custody of children should belong equally to both parents.
> That a man should be legally responsible for his illegitimate children.
> That he should be bound to maintain the woman he has wronged.

In the father of Mary Shelley we have another whose early life and antecedents must not be passed over. William Godwin, the seventh of thirteen children, was born at Wisbeach, Cambridgeshire, on March 3, 1756. He was naturally, to a great extent, a follower of Rousseau, and a sympathiser with the ideas of the French Revolution. Among Godwin's multifarious writings are his novels, some of which had great success, especially *Caleb Williams*. With Godwin and Wollstonecraft friendship melted into love, and they were married shortly afterwards, in March 1797, at old St. Pancras Church, London. But, alas! this loving married friendship was not to last long. On August 30, 1797, Mary was born, not the William so quaintly spoken of. Within a few hours of the child's birth, dangerous symptoms began with the mother; ten days of dread anxiety ensued, and not all the care of intelligent watchers, nor the constant waiting for service of the husband's faithful intimate friends, nor the skill of the first doctors could save the life which was doomed.

Of anecdotes of Mary's infancy and childhood there are but few, but by all accounts she was a happy child despite the loss of her mother. In 1801 Godwin accepted the demonstrative advances of Mrs Clairmont, a widow who took up her residence next door to him in the Polygon, Somers Town. She had two children, a boy and a girl, the latter somewhat younger than Mary. The widow needed no introduction or admittance to his house, as from the balcony she was able to commence a campaign of flattery to which Godwin soon succumbed. The marriage took place in December 1801, at Shoreditch Church, and was not made known to Godwin's friends till after it had been solemnised. Mrs. Clairmont evidently did her best to help Godwin through the pecuniary difficulties of his career.

Mary's first son, William was born on January 24, 1816, yet was destined to be only for a few short years the joy of his parents, and then to rest in Rome, where Shelley was not long in following him.

We now (May 3, 1816) find Shelley, Mary, and Claire at Dover, again on a journey to Switzerland. From Dover Shelley wrote a kind letter to Godwin, explaining money matters, and promising to do all he could to help him. They pass by Paris, then by Troyes, Dijon, and Dôle, through the Jura range. This time is graphically described by Shelley in letters appended to the Six Weeks' Tour; the journey and the eight days' excursion in Switzerland. We read of the terrific changes of nature, the thunderstorms, one of which was more imposing than all the others, lighting up lake and pine forests with the most vivid brilliancy, and then nothing but blackness with rolling thunder. They return by July 28 to Montalègre, where Shelley writes of the collection of seeds he has been making, and which Mary intends cultivating in her garden in England.

For another month these young restless beings enjoy the calm of their cottage by the lake, close to the Villa Diodati, while the poets breathe in poetry on all sides, and give it to the world in verse. Mary notes the books they read, and their visits in the evening to Diodati, where she became accustomed to the sound of Byron's voice, with Shelley's always the answering echo, for she was too awed and timid to speak much herself. These conversations caused her, subsequently, when hearing Byron's voice, to feel a sad want for 'the sound of a voice that is still.'

It is during this sojourn by the Swiss Lake that Mary began her first serious attempt at literature. Being asked each day by Shelley whether she had found a story, she answered 'No,' till one evening after listening to a conversation between Byron and Shelley on the principle of life - whether it would be discovered, and the power of communicating life be acquired - 'perhaps a corpse might be reanimated; galvanism had given tokens of such things' - she lay awake, and with the sound of the lake and the sight of the moonlight gleaming through chinks in the shutters, were blended the idea and the figure of a student engaged in the ghastly work of creating a man, until such a horror came to light that he shrank in fear from his own performance. Such was the original idea for this imaginative work of a girl of nineteen, which has held its place among conspicuous works of fiction to the present day. *Frankenstein* was the outcome of the project before mentioned of writing tales of horror. One night, when pouring rain detained Shelley's party at the Villa Diodati over a blazing fire, they told strange stories, till Byron, leading to poetic ideas, recited the witch's scene from 'Christabel,' which so excited Shelley's imagination that he shrieked, and ran from the room; and Polidori writes that he brought him to by throwing water in his face. Upon his reviving, they agreed to write each a supernatural tale. Matthew Gregory Lewis, the author of *The Monk*, who visited at Diodati, assisted them with these weird fancies.

That a work by a girl of nineteen should have held its place in romantic literature so long is no small tribute to its merit; this work, wrought under the influence of Byron and Shelley, and conceived after drinking in their enthralling conversation, is not unworthy of its origin. A more fantastically horrible story could scarcely be conceived; in fact, the vivid imagination, piling impossible horror upon horror, seems to claim for the book a place in the company of a Poe or a Hoffmann. Its weakness appears to be that of placing such an idea in the annals of modern life; such a process invariably weakens these powerful imaginative ideas, and takes away from, instead of adding to, the apparent truth, and cannot fail to give an affectation to the work. True, it might add to the difficulty to imagine a different state of society, past or future, but this seems a *sine quâ non*. The story of *Frankenstein* begins with a series of letters of a young man, Robert Walton, writing to his sister, Mrs. Saville in England, from St. Petersburg, where he is about to embark on a voyage in search of the North Pole. He is bent on discovering the secret of the magnet, and is deluded with the hope of a never absent sun. When advanced some distance towards his longed-for goal, Walton writes of a most strange adventure which befalls them in the midst of the ice regions a gigantic being, of human shape, being drawn over the ice in a sledge by dogs. Not many hours after this strange sight a fresh discovery was made of another man in another sledge, with only one living dog to it: this time the man was seen to be a European, whom the sailors tried to persuade to enter their ship. On seeing Walton the stranger, speaking English, asked whither they were bound before he would consent to enter the ship. This naturally caused intense excitement, as the man, reduced to a skeleton, seemed to have but a short time to live. However, on hearing that the vessel was bound northwards, he consented to enter, and with great care he was restored for the time. In answer to an inquiry as to his object in thus exposing himself, he replied, 'To seek one who fled from me.' An affection springs up and increases between Walton and the stranger, till the latter promises to tell his sad and strange story, which he had hitherto intended should die with him.

This commencement leads to the story being told in the form (which might with advantage have been avoided) of a long narrative by the dying man. The stranger describes himself as of a Genevese family of high distinction, and gives an interesting account of his father and juvenile surroundings, including a playfellow, Elizabeth Lavenga, whom we encounter much later in his history. All his studies are pursued with zest, till coming upon the works of Cornelius Agrippa he is led with enthusiasm into the ideas of experimental philosophy; a passing remark of 'trash' from his father, who does not explain the difference between past and modern science, is not enough to deter him and prevent the fatal consequence of the study he persists in, and thus a pupil of Albertus Magnus appears in the eighteenth century. The effects of a thunderstorm, described from those Mary had recently witnessed, decided him in his resolution, for electricity now was the aim of his research.

After having passed his youth in his happy Swiss home with his parents and dear friends, on the death of his loved mother he starts for the University of Ingolstadt. Here he is much reprehended by the professors for his useless studies, until one, a Mr. Waldeman, sympathises with him, and explains how Cornelius Agrippa and others, although their studies did not bring the immediate fruit they expected, nevertheless helped on science in other directions, and he advises Frankenstein to pursue his studies in natural philosophy, including mathematics. The upshot of this advice is that two years are spent in intense study and thought, till he becomes thin and haggard in appearance. He is contemplating a visit to his home, when, making some fresh experiment, he finds that he has discovered the principle of life; this so overcomes him for a time that, oblivious of all else, he is bent on making use of his discovery. After much perplexing thought he determines to create a being superior to man, so that future generations shall bless him. In the first place, by the help of chemistry, he has to construct the form which is to be animated. The grave has to be ransacked in the attempt, and Frankenstein describes with loathing some of the details of his work, and shows the danger of overstraining the mind in any one direction - how the virtuous become vicious, and how virtue itself, carried to excess, lapses into vice.

The form is created in nervous fear and fever. Frankenstein being the ideal scientist, devoid of all feeling for art (whose ideas of it, indeed, might be limited to the elevation and section of a pot), without any ideal of proportion or beauty, reaches the point where he considers nothing but the infusion of life necessary. All is ready, and in the first hour of the morning he applies his fatal discovery. Breath is given, the limbs move, the eyes open, and the colossal being or monster, as he is henceforth called, becomes animated; though copied from statues, its fearful size, its terrible complexion and drawn skin, scarcely concealing arteries and muscles beneath, add to the horror of the expression. And this is the end of two years work to the horrified Frankenstein. Overwhelmed by disgust, he can only rush from the room, and finally falls exhausted on his bed, only to wake to find his monster grinning at him. He runs forth into the street, and here, in Mary's first work, we have a reminiscence of her own infant days, when she and Claire hid themselves under the sofa to hear Coleridge read his poem, for the following stanza from the *Ancient Mariner* might seem almost the key-note of *Frankenstein*:

Like one who on a lonely road, Doth walk in fear and dread, And having once turned round, walks on, And turns no more his head, Because he knows a fearful fiend Doth close behind him tread.

Frankenstein hurries on, but coming across his old friend Henri Clerval at the stage coach, he recalls to mind his father, Elizabeth, his former life and friends. He returns to his rooms with his friend. Reaching his door, he trembles, but opening it, finds himself delivered from his self-created fiend. His frenzy of delight being attributed to madness from overwork, Clerval induces Frankenstein to leave his studies, and, finally (after he had for months endured a terrible illness), to accompany him to his native village. Various delays occurring, they are detained too late in the year to pass the dangerous roads on their way home.

Health and peace of mind returning to some degree, Frankenstein is about to proceed on his journey homewards, when a letter arrives from his father with the fatal news of the mysterious death of his young brother. This event hastens still further his return, and gives a renewed gloomy turn to his mind; not only is his loved little brother dead, but the extraordinary event points to some unknown power. From this time Frankenstein's life is one agony. One after another all whom he loves fall victims to the demon he has created; he is never safe from his presence; in a storm on the Alps he encounters him; in the fearful murders which annihilate his family he always recognises his hand.

On one occasion his creation wished to have a truce and to come to terms with his creator. This, after his most fearful treachery had caused the innocent to be sentenced as the perpetrator of his fearful deeds. On meeting Frankenstein he recounts the most pathetic story of his falling away from sympathy with humanity: how, after saving the life of a girl from drowning, he is shot by a young man who rushes up and rescues her from him. He became the unknown benefactor of a family for some period of time by doing the hard work of the household while they slept. Having taking refuge in a hovel adjoining a corner of their cottage, he hears their pathetic and romantic story, and also learns the language and ways of men; but on his wishing to make their acquaintance the family are so horrified at his appearance that the women faint, the men drive him off with blows, and the whole family leave a

---

70

neighbourhood, the scene of such an apparition. After these experiences he retaliates, till meeting Frankenstein he proposes these terms: that Frankenstein shall create another being as repulsive as himself to be his companion - in fact, he desires a wife as hideous as he is. These were the conditions, and the lives of all those whom Frankenstein held most dear were in the balance; he hesitated long, but finally consented.

Everything now had to be put aside to carry out this fearful task - his love of Elizabeth, his father's entreaties that he should marry her, his hopes, his ambitions, go for nothing. To save those who remain, he must devote himself to his work. To carry out his aim he expresses a wish to visit England, and, with his friend Clerval, descends the Rhine, which is described with the knowledge gained in Mary's own journey, and the same route is pursued which she, Shelley, and Claire had taken through Holland, embarking for England from Rotterdam, and thence reaching the Thames. After passing London and Oxford and various places of interest, he expresses a desire to be left for a time in solitude, and selects a remote island of the Orkneys, where an uninhabited hut answers the purpose of his laboratory. Here he works unmolested till his fearful task is nearly accomplished, when a fear and loathing possess his soul at the possible result of this second achievement. Although the demon already created has sworn to abandon the haunts of man and to live in a desert country with his mate, what hold will there be over this second being with an individuality and will of its own? What might be the future consequences to humanity of the existence of such monsters?

He forms a resolution to abandon his dreaded work, and at that moment it is confirmed by the sight of his monster grinning at him through the window of the hut in the moonlight. Not a moment is lost. He tears his just completed work limb from limb. The monster disappears in rage, only to return to threaten eternal revenge on him and his; but the time of weakness is passed; better encounter any evils that may be in store, even for those he loves, than leave a curse to humanity. From that time there is no truce. Clerval is murdered and Frankenstein is seized as the murderer, but respited for worse fate; he is married to Elizabeth, and she is strangled within a few hours. When goaded to the verge of madness by all these events, and seeing his beloved father reduced to imbecility through their misfortunes, he can make no one believe his self-accusing story; and if they did, what would it avail to pursue a being who could scale the Alps, live among glaciers, and pass unfathomable seas?

There is nothing left but a pursuit till death, single-handed, when one might expire and the other be appeased - onward, with a deluding sight from time to time of his avenging demon. Only in sleep and dreams did Frankenstein find forgetfulness of his self-imposed torture, for he lived again with those he had loved; he endured life in his pursuit by imagining his waking hours to be a horrible dream and longing for the night, when sleep should bring him life. When hopes of meeting his demon failed, some fresh trace would appear to lead him on through habited and uninhabited countries; he tracks him to the verge of the eternal ice, and even there procures a sledge from the wretched and horrified inhabitants of the last dwelling-place of men to pursue the monster, who, on a similar vehicle, had departed, to their delight. Onwards, onwards, over the eternal ice they pass, the pursued and the pursuer, till consciousness is nearly lost, and Frankenstein is rescued by those to whom he now narrates his history; all except his fatal scientific secret, which is to die with him shortly, for the end cannot be far off.

The story is told, and the friend - for he feels the utmost sympathy with the tortures of Frankenstein - can only attempt to soothe his last days or hours, for he, too, feels the end must be near; but at this crisis in Frankenstein's existence the expedition cannot proceed northward, for the crew mutiny to return. Frankenstein determines to proceed alone; but his strength is ebbing, and Walton foresees his early death. But this is not to pass quietly, for the demon is in no mood that his creator should escape unmolested from his grasp. Now the time is ripe, and, during a momentary absence, Walton is startled by fearful sounds, and then, in the cabin of his dying friend, a sight to appal the bravest; for the fiend is having the death struggle with him - then all is over. Some last speeches of the demon to Walton are explanatory of his deed, and of his present intention of self-immolation, as he has now slaked his thirst to wreak vengeance for his existence. Then he disappears over the ice to accomplish this last task.

Surely there is enough weird imagination for the subject. Mary in this work not merely intended to depict the horror of such a monster, but she evidently wished also to show what a being, with no naturally bad propensities, might sink to when under the influence of a false position - the education of Rousseau's natural man not being here possible.

Some weak points, some incongruities, it would be unreasonable not to expect. Whether the *eternal* light expected at the North Pole, if of the sun, was a misapprehension of the author or a Shelleyan application of the word eternal (as applied by him to certain friendships, or duration of residence in houses) may be questioned. The question as to the form used for the narrative has already been referred to. The difficulty of such a method is strangely exemplified in the long letters which are quoted by Frankenstein to his friend while dying, and which he could not have carried with him on his deadly pursuit. Mary's facility in writing was great, and having visited some of the most interesting places in the world, with some of the most interesting people, she is saved from the dreary dullness of the dull. Her ideas, also, though sometimes affected, are genuine, not the outcome of some fashionable foible to please a passing faith or superstition, which ought never to be the *raison d'etre* of a romance, though it may be of a satire or a sermon.

The last passage in the book is perhaps the weakest. It is scarcely the climax, but an anticlimax. The end of *Frankenstein* is well conceived, but that of the Demon fails. It is ridiculous to conceive anyone, demon or human, having ended his vengeance, fleeing over the ice to burn himself on a funeral pyre where no fuel could be found. Surely the tortures of the lowest pit of Dante's *Inferno* might have sufficed for the occasion. The youth of the authoress of this remarkable romance has raised comparison between it and the first work of a still younger romancist, the author of *Gabriel Denver*, written at seventeen, who died before he had completed his twentieth year.

While this romance was being planned during the latter part of the stay of the Shelley party in Switzerland, after their return from Chamouni, the diary gives us a charming idea of their life in their cottage of Montalègre. We have the books they read, as usual; and well did Mary, no less than Shelley, make use of that happy reading-time of life: youth. The Latin authors read by Shelley were also studied by Mary. We find her reading 'Quintus Curtius,' ten and twelve pages at a time; also on Shelley's birthday, August 4, she reads him the fourth book of Virgil, while in a boat with him on the lake. Also the fire-balloon is not forgotten, which Mary had made two or three days in advance for the occasion. They used generally to visit Diodati in the evening, after dinner, though occasionally Shelley dined with Byron, and accompanied him in his boat. On one occasion Mary wrote: 'Shelley and Claire go up to Diodati; I do not, for Lord Byron did not seem to wish it.' Rousseau, Voltaire, and other authors cause the time to fly, until their spirits are damped by a letter arriving from Shelley's solicitor, requiring his return to England.

While in Switzerland Mary received some letters from Fanny, her half-sister; these letters are interesting, showing a sweet, gentle disposition, very affectionate to both Shelley and Mary. One letter asks Mary questions about Lord Byron. There are also details as to the unfortunate state of the finances of Godwin, who seemed in a perennial state of needing three hundred pounds. Fanny also writes of herself, on July 29, 1816, as not being well - being in a state of mind which always keeps her body in a fever - her lonely life, after her sister's departure, with all the money anxieties, and her own dependence, evidently weighed upon her mind, and led to a state of despondency, although her letters would scarcely give the idea of a tragedy being imminent.

On leaving the Lake of Geneva on August 28 the party of three returned towards England by way of Dijon, and thence by a different route from that by which they had gone, returning by Rouvray, Auxerre, Fontainebleau, and Versailles. Here Mary and Shelley visited the palace and town, which a few years hence she would revisit under far different circumstances. Travelling - in those days so very unlike what it is in ours, when Europe can be crossed without being examined - allowed them to become acquainted with the towns they passed through. Rouen was visited; but for some reason they were disappointed with the cathedral. Prom Havre they sailed for Portsmouth, when, with their usual fate, they encountered a stormy passage of twenty-seven hours.

Work was the great resource. Mary was writing her *Frankenstein*. She persisted with the utmost fortitude in intellectual employment, as poor Fanny wrote to Mary on September 26: 'I cannot help envying your calm, contented disposition, and the calm philosophical habits of life which pursue yon; or, rather, which you pursue everywhere; I allude to your description of the manner in which you pass your days at Bath, when most women would hardly have recovered from the fatigues of such a journey as you had been taking.'

This is, indeed, the key-note of Mary's character, which, with her sensitive, retiring nature, enabled her to live through the stormy times of her life with equanimity.

Mary had Shelley's company through November, but at the beginning of December she writes to Shelley, who is again staying with Peacock house-hunting. Mary tells him what she would like: 'A house (with a lawn) near a river or lake, noble trees, or divine mountains'. Mary also tells, what is more interesting, that she has finished the fourth chapter, a very long one, of her *Frankenstein*, which she thinks Shelley will like. She wishes for his return.

The death of Harriet was necessarily quickly followed by the marriage of Shelley and Mary. The most sound opinions were ascertained as to the desirability of an early marriage, or of postponing the ceremony for a year after the death of Harriet; all agreed that the wedding ought to take place without delay, and it was fixed for December 30, 1816, at St. Mildred's Church in the City, where Godwin and his wife were present, to their no little satisfaction, as described by

Shelley to Claire.

On May 14 1817 we find Mary has finished and corrected her *Frankenstein*, and she decides to go to London and stay with her father while carrying on the negotiations with Murray whom she wishes to publish it. Shelley accompanies Mary for a few days at Godwin's invitation, but returns to look after 'Blue Eyes,' to whom he is charged with a million kisses from Mary. But Mary returns speedily to Shelley and 'Blue Eyes,' having felt very restless while absent. She soon falls into a plan of Shelley's for partially adopting a little Polly who frequently spent the day or slept in their house, and Mary would find time to tell her before she went to bed whatever she or Shelley had been reading that day, always asking her what she thought of it.

Mary, who was expecting another child in the autumn, was not long idle after the completion of *Frankenstein*, but set to work copying and revising her Six Weeks' Tour. This work, begun in August, she completed after the birth of her baby Clara on September 2. In October the book was bought and later published by Hookham.

The Life and Letters of Mary Shelley by J Marshall (1889)

The following excerpts taken from *The Life and Letters of Mary Shelley* include the writer's own account of how novel came to be written.

The list of books read during 1815 by Mary Shelley is worth appending, as giving some idea of their wonderful mental activity and insatiable thirst for knowledge, and the singular sympathy which existed between them in these intellectual pursuits. Those marked * were also read by Shelley.

Posthumous Works. 3 vols. / Sorrows of Werter. / Don Roderick. By Southey. / *Gibbon's Decline and Fall 12 vols. / *Gibbon's Life and Letters. 1st Edition. 2 vols. / *Lara. / New Arabian Knights. 3 vols. / Corinna. / Fall of the Jesuits. / Rinaldo Rinaldini. / Fontenelle's Plurality of Worlds. / Hermsprong. / Le Diable Boiteux. / Man as he is. / Rokeby. / Ovid's Metamorphoses in Latin. / *Wordsworth's Poems. / *Spenser's Fairy Queen. / *Life of the Phillips. / *Fox's History of James II. / The Reflector. / Fleetwood. / Wieland. / Don Carlos. / *Peter Wilkins. / Rousseau's Confessions. / Leonora: a Poem. / Emile. / *Milton's Paradise Lost. / *Life of Lady Hamilton. / De l'Allemagne. By Madame de Staël. / Three vols, of Barruet. / *Caliph Vathek. / Nouvelle Heloise. / *Kotzebue's Account of his Banishment to Siberia. / Waverley. / Clarissa Harlowe. / Robertson's History of America. / *Virgil. / *Tale of a Tub. / *Milton's Speech on Unlicensed Printing. / *Curse of Kehama. / *Madoc. / La Bible Expliquée. / Lives of Abelard and Heloise. / *The New Testament. / *Coleridge's Poems. / First vol. of Système de la Nature. / Castle of Indolence. / Chatterton's Poems. / *Paradise Regained. / Don Carlos. / *Lycidas. / *St. Leon. / Shakespeare's Plays (part of which Shelley read aloud). / *Burke's Account of Civil Society. / *Excursion. / Pope's Homer's Illiad. / *Sallust. / Micromejas. / *Life of Chaucer. / Canterbury Tales. / Peruvian Letters. / Voyages round the World. / Plutarch's Lives. / *Two vols, of Gibbon. / Ormond. /

Hugh Trevor. / *Labaume's History of the Russian War. /
Lewis's Tales. / Castle of Udolpho. / Guy Mannering. /
*Charles XII by Voltaire. / Tales of the East.

To the intellectual ferment, so to speak, of the
Diodati evenings, working with the new experiences and
thoughts of the past two years, is due the conception of the
story by which, as a writer, she is best remembered, the ghastly
but powerful allegorical romance of *Frankenstein*. In her
introduction to a late edition of this work Mary Shelley has
herself told the history of its origin:

In the summer of 1816 we visited Switzerland, and
became the neighbours of Lord Byron. At first we spent our
pleasant hours on the lake, or wandering on its shores, and
Lord Byron, who was writing the third canto of *Childe Harold*,
was the only one among us who put his thoughts upon paper.
These, as he brought them successively to us, clothed in all the
light and harmony of poetry, seemed to stamp as divine the
glories of heaven and earth, whose influences we partook with
him.

But it proved a wet, ungenial summer, and incessant
rain often confined us for days to the house. Some volumes of
ghost stories, translated from the German into French, fell into
our hands. There was the history of the Inconstant Lover, who,
when he thought to clasp the bride to whom he had pledged his
vows, found himself in the arms of the pale ghost of her whom
he had deserted. There was the tale of the sinful founder of his
race, whose miserable doom it was to bestow the kiss of death
on all the younger sons of his fated house, just when they
reached the age of promise. His gigantic shadowy form,
clothed, like the ghost in Hamlet, in complete armour, but with
the beaver up, was seen at midnight, by the moon's fitful
beams, to advance slowly along the gloomy avenue. The shape
was lost beneath the shadow of the castle walls; but soon a
gate swung back, a step was heard, the door of the chamber
opened, and he advanced to the couch of the blooming youths,
cradled in healthy sleep. Eternal sorrow sat upon his face as he

---

bent down and kissed the forehead of the boys, who from that hour withered like flowers snapt upon the stalk. I have not seen these stories since then, but their incidents are as fresh in my mind as if I had read them yesterday. "We will each write a ghost story," said Byron; and his proposition was acceded to. There were four of us. The noble author began a tale, a fragment of which he printed at the end of his poem of Mazeppa. Shelley, more apt to embody ideas and sentiments in the radiance of brilliant imagery, and in the music of the most melodious verse that adorns our language, than to invent the machinery of a story, commenced one founded on the experiences of his early life. Poor Polidori had some terrible idea about a skull-headed lady, who was so punished for peeping through a keyhole - what to see I forget, something very shocking and wrong of course; but when she was reduced to a worse condition than the renowned Tom of Coventry he did not know what to do with her, and he was obliged to despatch her to the tomb of the Capulets, the only place for which she was fitted. The illustrious poets also, annoyed by the platitude of prose, speedily relinquished their ungrateful task. I busied myself to think of a story, a story to rival those which had excited us to this task. One that would speak to the mysterious fears of our nature, and awaken thrilling horror - one to make the reader dread to look round, to curdle the blood and quicken the beatings of the heart. If I did not accomplish these things my ghost story would be unworthy of its name. I thought and wondered - vainly. I felt that blank incapability of invention which is the greatest misery of authorship, when dull Nothing replies to our anxious invocations. 'Have you thought of a story?' I was asked each morning, and each morning I was forced to reply with a mortifying negative.

Many and long were the conversations between Lord Byron and Shelley, to which I was a devout but nearly silent listener. During one of these various philosophical doctrines were discussed, and, among others, the nature of the principle of life, and whether there was any probability of its ever being discovered and communicated. They talked of the experiments of Dr. Darwin (I speak not of what the doctor really did, or said that he did, but, as more to my purpose, of what was then spoken of as having been done by him), who preserved a piece of vermicelli in a glass case till by some extraordinary means it began to move with voluntary motion. Not thus, after all, would life be given. Perhaps a corpse would be reanimated; galvanism had given token of such things; perhaps the component parts of a Creature might be manufactured, brought together, and endued with vital warmth.

Night waned upon this talk, and even the witching hour had gone by, before we retired to rest. When I placed my head upon my pillow I did not sleep, nor could I be said to think. My imagination, unbidden, possessed and guided me, gifting the successive images that arose in my mind with a vividness far beyond the usual bounds of reverie. I saw with shut eyes, but acute mental vision, I saw the pale student of unhallowed arts kneeling beside the thing he had put together - I saw the hideous phantasm of a man stretched out, and then, on the working of some powerful engine, show signs of life, and stir with an uneasy, half vital motion. Frightful must it be; for supremely frightful would be the effect of any human endeavour to mock the stupendous mechanism of the Creator of the world. His success would terrify the artist; he would rush away from his odious handiwork, horrorstricken. He would hope that, left to itself, the slight spark which he had communicated would fade; that this thing, which had received such imperfect animation, would subside into dead matter; and he might sleep in the belief that the silence of the grave would quench for ever the transient existence of the hideous corpse which he had looked upon as the cradle of life. He sleeps; but he is awakened; he opens his eyes; behold the horrid thing stands at his bedside, opening his curtains, and looking on him with yellow, watery, but speculative eyes.

I opened mine in terror. The idea so possessed my mind that a thrill of fear ran through me, and I wished to exchange the ghastly image of my fancy for the realities around. I see them still; the very room, the dark parquet, the closed shutters, with the moonlight struggling through, and the sense I had that the glassy lake and white high Alps were

---

beyond. I could not so easily get rid of my hideous phantom; still it haunted me. I must try to think of something else. I recurred to my ghost story - my tiresome unlucky ghost story. O! if I could only contrive one which would frighten my reader as I myself had been frightened that night!

Swift as light and as cheering was the idea that broke in upon me. 'I have found it! What terrified me will terrify others; and I need only describe the spectre which had haunted my midnight pillow.' On the morrow I announced that I had *thought of a story*. I began that day with the words, *It was on a dreary night of November*, making only a transcript of the grim terrors of my waking dream.

At first I thought of but a few pages of a short tale; but Shelley urged me to develop the idea at greater length. I certainly did not owe the suggestion of one incident, nor scarcely of one train of feeling, to my husband, and yet, but for his incitement, it would never have taken the form in which it was presented to the world.

* * * * *

Every one now knows the story of the 'Modern Prometheus', the student who, having devoted himself to the search for the principle of life, discovers it, manufactures an imitation of a human being, endows it with vitality, and having thus encroached on divine prerogative, finds himself the slave of his own Creature, for he has set in motion a force beyond his power to control or annihilate. Aghast at the actual and possible consequences of his own achievement, he recoils from carrying it out to its ultimate end, and stops short of doing what is necessary to render this force independent. The being has, indeed, the perception and desire of goodness; but is, by the circumstances of its abnormal existence, delivered over to evil, and Frankenstein, and all whom he loves, fall victims to its vindictive malice. Surely no girl, before or since, has imagined, and carried out to its pitiless conclusion so grim an idea.

Mary began her rough sketch of this story during the

absence of Shelley and Byron on a voyage round the lake of Geneva; the memorable excursion during which Byron wrote the *Prisoner of Chillon*. When they returned they found Mary hard at work on the fantastic speculation which possessed her mind and exerted over it a fascination and a power of excitement beyond that of the sublime external nature which inspired the two poets.

When, in July, she set off with Shelley and Clare on a short tour to the Valley of Chamounix, she took her MS. with her. They visited the Mer de Glace, and the source of the Arveiron. The magnificent scenery which inspired Shelley with his poem on "Mont Blanc," and is described by Mary in the extracts from her journal which follow, served her as a fitting background for the most preternatural portions of her romance.

Tuesday, July 23 (Chamounix). In the morning, after breakfast, we mount our mules to see the source of the Arveiron. When we had gone about three parts of the way, we descended and continued our route on foot, over loose stones, many of which were an enormous size. We came to the source, which lies (like a stage) surrounded on the three sides by mountains and glaciers. We sat on a rock, which formed the fourth, gazing on the scene before us. An immense glacier was on our left, which continually rolled stones to its foot. It is very dangerous to be directly under this. Our guide told us a story of two Hollanders who went, without any guide, into a cavern of the glacier, and fired a pistol there, which drew down a large piece on them. We see several avalanches, some very small, others of great magnitude, which roared and smoked, overwhelming everything as it passed along, and precipitating great pieces of ice into the valley below. This glacier is increasing every day a foot, closing up the valley. We drink some water of the Arveiron and return. After dinner think it will rain, and Shelley goes alone to the glacier of Boison. I stay at home. Read several tales of Voltaire. In the evening I copy Shelley's letter to Peacock.

Wednesday, July 24 Today is rainy; therefore we

cannot go to Col de Balme. About 10 the weather appears clearing up. Shelley and I begin our journey to Montanvert. Nothing can be more desolate than the ascent of this mountain; the trees in many places having been torn away by avalanches, and some half leaning over others, intermingled with stones, present the appearance of vast and dreadful desolation. It began to rain almost as soon as we left our inn. When we had mounted considerably we turned to look on the scene. A dense white mist covered the vale, and tops of scattered pines peeping above were the only objects that presented themselves. The rain continued in torrents. We were wetted to the skin; so that, when we had ascended halfway, we resolved to turn back. As we descended, Shelley went before, and, tripping up, fell upon his knee. This added to the weakness occasioned by a blow on his ascent; he fainted, and was for some minutes incapacitated from continuing his route.

Friday, August 2 I go to the town with Shelley, to buy a telescope for his birthday present. In the evening Lord Byron and he go out in the boat, and, after their return, Shelley and Clare go up to Diodati; I do not, for Lord Byron did not seem to wish it. Shelley returns with a letter from Longdill, which requires his return to England. This puts us in bad spirits.

* * * * *

At the Bagni di Lucca, where they settled themselves for a time, Mary heard from her father of the review of *Frankenstein* in the *Quarterly*. Peacock had reported it to be unfavourable, so it was probably a relief to find that the reviewers "did not pretend to find anything blasphemous in the story." They say that the *gentleman* who has written the book is *a man of talents*, but that he employs his powers in a way disagreeable to them.

All this, however, tended to keep Mary's old ardour alive. She never was more strongly impelled to write than at this time; she felt her powers fresh and strong within her; all she wanted was some motive, some suggestion to guide her in

83

the choice of a subject. She was immensely attracted by the idea, but was forced to abandon it at the time, for lack of the necessary books of reference. But Shelley, who believed her powers to be of the highest order, was as eager as she herself could be for her to undertake original work of some kind, and was constantly inciting her to effort in this direction.

'There is nothing which the human mind can conceive which it may not execute.' Shakespeare was only a human being. Adieu till Thursday. Your ever affectionate, P. B. S.

Bibliography

Botting, Fred: *Gothic* (Routledge, 1996)
Nora Crook: A Companion to the Gothic (Wiley, 2001)
Day, Aidan: *Romanticism* (Routledge, 2001)
Michael Gamer: *Cambridge Companion to the Gothic* (Cambridge 2002)
Gonda, Caroline: Reading Daughters' Fictions 1709-1934 (Cambridge 1996)
Hemmings, F.W.J: *Romanticism and Realism* in *The Age of Realism* (The Harvester Press, 1978)
Kagarlitski, Julius: *Realism and Fantasy* in Thomas D. Clareson (ed.), *SF: The Other Side of Realism* (Bowling Green University Popular Press, 1971)
Mrs Julian Marshall: *The Life and Letters of Mary Wollstonecraft Shelley* (Bentley & Son 1889)
Shelley, Mary (1818): *Frankenstein* ed. Maurice Hindle (Penguin, 1992)

Printed in Great Britain
by Amazon

35957293R00048